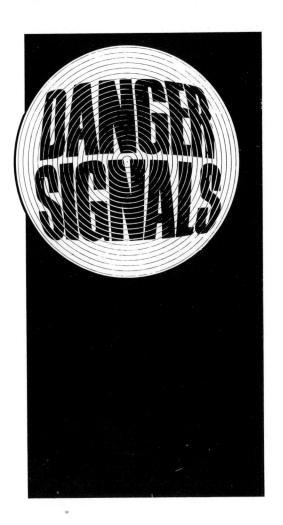

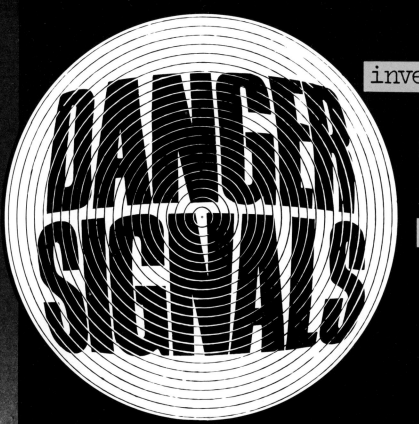

DANGER SIGNALS

An investigation into modern railway accidents

STANLEY HALL

LONDON

IAN ALLAN LTD

Contents

Previous page:
Bristol Temple Meads: a night view looking east into the spectacle of the colour-light signals from the end of Platform 9. Ian Allan Library

First published 1987

ISBN 0 7110 1704 2

Published by Ian Allan Ltd,
Shepperton, Surrey; and printed by
Ian Allan Printing Ltd at their works
at Coombelands in Runnymede,
England

Foreword

by
Major C. F. Rose MBE, C.Eng, FICE, MCIT,
Chief Inspecting Officer of Railways,
Department of Transport

Railway accidents are always news. Even relatively minor ones reach the front page, whilst more serious ones in other modes of transport might not be mentioned at all. In part this is a reflection of the railways' long history, but there is also the railways' success in achieving such high levels of safety; people do not expect trains to crash and when they do there is often a feeling of shock or bewilderment. However, we have to recognise that there will always be accidents, since there is no such thing as absolute safety. What is important is that the cause of most accidents that do occur is investigated in depth — and not only the immediate cause but also the underlying factors which may have set the scene for the accident. It is on these underlying factors that Stan Hall had concentrated and it is this that makes his book much more than just a catalogue of disasters. I believe that it will be read with interest and profit by professional railwaymen who, whilst they may not agree with all that is written, will find themselves challenged to think about aspects of safety that may have passed unnoticed or been dismissed as irrelevant. The informed amateur will be intrigued by the opportunity to look behind the scenes and follow the sometimes tortuous but always fascinating search for safety, and even those with little knowledge of railways should find much of interest, and reassurance, in the story that unfolds. Stan Hall's long experience as a railwayman, culminating in his position at the centre of British Railways' search for a railway that is efficient, economic and safe, has given him the credentials to write this book. In doing so, I believe he has made a positive contribution to the cause of railway safety.

Left:
Manchester Piccadilly — an orderly array of colour-light signalling amidst the confusion of overhead cables.
British Railways

Introduction

It could be said that I have been preparing this book for the last 40 years or so, ever since I started work with the London Midland & Scottish Railway in April 1943 at the age of 17 as a junior booking clerk at Keighley, on the Midland Division main line between Leeds and Carlisle. I quickly found that I was interested in railway operating, particularly signalling and safety, and in my spare time in those early days I was usually to be found somewhere around the station or in the signalboxes, of which there were no fewer than six. There were two serious accidents in the area about that time, 1943/44, to arouse my interest, one being the derailment on the curve at Thwaites, just south of Keighley, of a number of fish vans at the rear of one of the Up Scotch sleeping car expresses. The other was a collision at Steeton, just north of Keighley, when the Down Edinburgh sleeper crashed into a goods train being set back into the refuge siding. Being wartime, neither of these accidents received much publicity.

My first experience of a Ministry of Transport Public Inquiry was in 1948, when I went to the Crewe Arms Hotel to hear about the Winsford crash, which occurred when the Up Postal express ran into the back of the 5.40pm Glasgow-Euston, the latter being at a standstill after the communication cord had been pulled. Shortly after this I took the first step on the 'Operating' ladder with responsibilities for the safety of trains and passengers, when I became a station master at a small station in the industrial West Riding. The receipts hardly covered the porters' wages, and the station — Battyeford, on the Leeds-Huddersfield 'new' line — was not worth keeping open, but there were five signalboxes, including four on the very busy four-track section between Mirfield and Huddersfield, and it was a good training ground for someone interested in signalling and safety. By chance I discovered that the District Signalmen's Inspector had an extensive collection of Ministry of Transport accident reports, which he lent to me. I devoured them from cover to cover, and so began an admiration for the work and the Reports of the Inspecting Officers of the Ministry of Transport which has lasted to the present day. Throughout the remainder of my career with British Railways in many parts of the country, at station, division, and HQ level, I had responsibilities for safety and accident investigation, culminating in five years at British Railways Board Headquarters as the Signalling & Safety Officer. During that period, or in the preceding years, I managed to visit almost every power signalbox on BR, and had the good fortune to be able to travel in the driving cab, usually with an Inspector, over virtually every main line in Britain. During the course of this I met, and was able to discuss safety problems with, many hundreds of signalmen and drivers. I shall always be grateful to those who helped me to get a better 'feel' of what it is to be a driver or a signalman, and to be able to appreciate their problems and responsibilities. I never cease to be impressed by their quite proper pride in their craft, and their dedication to the railway. They need no lessons in customer care — the customer has always been their first concern.

Those, then, are my qualifications for writing this book. It is a book which I believe needed to be written, not just to explain how accidents happen but also *why* they happen despite the existence of modern safeguards and a great deal of expenditure. I expect that I may have trodden on a few toes in doing so and if I have unwittingly caused hurt or offence, I hope that my apologies will be accepted. I have tried to be objective throughout, not an easy task with the burden of 40 years' loyalty and tradition, and if I have failed in that objectivity the responsibility is mine, and mine alone. This book is in no way an official review of safety standards. The British Railways Board has hardly been involved at all in its preparation, except for the provision of a small amount of information, and that is the way both the Board and I have preferred it. Whilst I would have tried to be objective even with BR's co-operation in assembling the material, there would have been an inevitable suspicion that I was, even if in only a small

Below:
A scene that used to be repeated everywhere on Britain's railways during foggy weather or falling snow. The fog signalman placed a warning fog signal on the rail to explode when a train passed over it. His hut and brazier have now passed into railway history, together with his long overcoat, cloth cap and walrus moustache. Ian Allan Library

Left:
An instructor explains the functions of a signal at Willesden to two drivers during a tour of the yards and sidings.
British Railways (LMR)

measure, presenting the BR case. Happily, that eventuality has not arisen.

Some may feel that my criticisms of railway management are too restrained and that, on the facts I have presented, a harsher criticism would have been justified. Others may take the opposite view. I can only leave readers to judge for themselves. At the same time I have been anxious not to let hindsight colour my judgement, a trap into which it would be very easy to fall. It must also be remembered that a thousand trains arriving safely is not news; the one that does not is. The book deals mainly with recent serious accidents, and then only those with an 'operating' flavour. In general, each chapter considers a different type of accident, and I make no apology for describing accidents in dramatic terms — accidents *are* dramatic — but I have deliberately avoided naming the people involved, because most of them are still alive.

In my descriptions of railway operating procedures, equipment, Rules, etc, I have tried to steer a middle course between long, tedious descriptions on the one hand, which might bore the professional railwayman or knowledgeable amateur, and a degree of brevity on the other hand, which might confuse the layman. The book is not aimed specially at railwaymen, although I hope that they might find it interesting and perhaps of value, but rather at the general public who are often curious to know just how railway accidents are caused, but find technical descriptions of railway procedures a little baffling. I have been anxious not

to take the reader's knowledge for granted, and if I have erred too far the other way I ask for your indulgence.

The basis of the book is an examination of the reasons behind the obvious causes of an accident. It is not enough to say that a driver, for example, made an error. One has to ask whether that error could (and should) have been foreseen, what preventive measures or equipment existed, whether more could have been done, and if so, why it had not been done. The research into these questions has been greatly facilitated by the availability of reports on all serious accidents, published by the Ministry of Transport following Public Inquiries held by Inspecting Officers. I am greatly indebted to the Chief Inspecting Officer, Major C. F. Rose MBE, who has readily placed his library of reports at my disposal. My working relationships with Major Rose and his fellow Inspecting Officers have been amongst the most enjoyable and rewarding of my railway career.

I am also indebted to the following for checking the script and for their helpful comments: Mr K. C. Appleby, former Area Manager at York, Mr T. Morgan, a main line driver at Skipton depot, and Mr J. E. Whitehouse MBE, former Divisional Staff Officer at Birmingham. My family and friends have given me unfailing support and encouragement, for which I am extremely grateful.

The utmost care has been taken to ensure factual accuracy as far as possible, but if any errors are detected I should be grateful to be informed. The opinions expressed are mine alone, and I take responsibility for them.

Safety at Signals and the Value of AWS

A few miles west of Manchester, the railway line from Liverpool and the M602 motorway run side by side. Drivers on the M602, faced with all the normal hazards of motorway driving, must often have looked enviously at trains passing in such effortless safety on the adjacent railway and wished that they could change places with the engine driver. Driving a train looks so easy; the signalman does all the steering, and all the driver has to do is stop when required. Or so it must have seemed until the morning of 4 December 1984, when those same motorway drivers were suddenly confronted with a ball of flame spreading across from the railway line, and were showered with burning debris. The 10.05 express Liverpool-Scarborough had plunged into the back of an almost stationary loaded oil tank train at 45-50mph. By great good fortune the front two coaches, which were engulfed in flames, were almost empty and only two passengers were killed, in addition to the driver. It is a tribute to modern coach design and construction that none of the other 150 passengers suffered serious injury.

The cause of the accident was quite clear — the driver passed Eccles Distant signal, which was giving a 'Caution' message, and the Home signal, which was saying 'Danger, Stop', without any apparent reaction, and his train continued forward at unchecked speed until a few seconds before it hit the oil tank train. Why the driver failed to react to the signals will never be known; he was killed at once.

The history of railways is littered with similar crashes, which may indicate that driving a train is perhaps not quite so simple as it looks. The driver must watch out for, and obey, every signal. He must always be on the alert and must never lose his concentration for an instant. It is a tribute to the sense of responsibility and self-discipline of drivers that there are so few lapses of concentration, and when the driver is killed in an accident of this nature it cannot be proved beyond doubt, but can only be assumed, that a lapse of concentration has taken place.

Faced with the likely consequences of human error of this nature, the railways have for many years sought and applied ways and means of guarding against it, and the

Below left:
Tragedy at Eccles. Class 45 locomotive No 45147 is seen here embedded in the rear of the oil tank train into which it crashed at speed on the morning of 4 December 1984, after having run past Eccles Home signal, which was at Danger. A. Sherratt

Bottom left:
Eccles: the burnt-out leading coach of the 10.05 express from Liverpool to Scarborough.
Manchester Evening News

Right:
Another view of the Eccles collision, looking westwards. Having the motorway alongside greatly facilitated the access of the rescue and emergency services. The foam used to fight the fire can clearly be seen.
Roger Kaye

Below:
Eccles: a huge road-transported heavy-lifting crane was used, almost dwarfing the railway breakdown crane beyond.
A. Sherratt

Below:
Eccles Up Home signal, seen in 1978, with the 11.56 Filey-Liverpool entering the station on the Down main line. This picture shows how the signal merges with the bridge beyond it.
Noel Johnston

Below right:
The same signal in August 1986, having been provided with a white back-plate to enable drivers to see it more easily. The DMU entering Eccles station is the 12.50 Manchester-Liverpool.
Author

question has to be asked as to why there were no such safeguards at Eccles signalbox. As long as a century ago much thought and ingenuity were being expended on the subject. An interesting experiment was then being conducted at Wimbledon on the London & South Western Railway using an apparatus similar to that later adopted by the Great Western Railway. It consisted of a bar lying between the rails at the Distant signal. When the signal was not in the 'Clear' position, the bar was raised slightly and made contact with a wheel-operated vertical rod on the underside of the locomotive, causing a whistle to sound. This system, known as Kempe & Rowell's patent, was primarily designed to enable the use of fog-signalmen to be discontinued, rather than as a means of assisting the driver in all weathers. Fog-signalling was an occupation attended with some danger, and was expensive. But Kempe could see the value of his and Rowell's apparatus as an additional all-weather safeguard for the driver. There was, however, a school of thought which held the view that nothing should

be done that might in any way distract the driver from his primary duty of observing and obeying signals, and that any mechanical or other aids might eventually and unwittingly lead to a reduction in his overall level of concentration. It was a view that was to prevail in some quarters for another half century and more, but there were exceptions, the Great Western being the most notable. Following a serious collision at Slough in June 1900, when the 1.15pm express from Paddington to Falmouth ran into the back of a passenger train standing in the station after the driver of the express had failed to obey the Distant signals, the Great Western considered what ought to be done to prevent a repetition, following prompting by Col Sir Arthur Yorke in his Report.

In January 1906 experimental apparatus was installed on one of its branch lines. The apparatus was similar to Kempe & Rowell's patent but with the warning being actuated electrically. Instead of the bar between the two rails being raised and lowered, a fixed ramp was provided which made

contact with a spring-loaded shoe on the locomotive. When the Distant signal was 'Clear' an electric current passed through the ramp and rang a bell on the locomotive. When the Distant signal was at 'Caution' no current passed and the raising of the spring-loaded shoe broke an electrical circuit and sounded an alarm. It was thus fail-safe; a fundamental principle of all signalling and safety equipment. The experiment was extended to the line between Paddington and Reading between 1908 and 1910 and the equipment was developed to provide an automatic application of the brake unless the driver intervened. The experiment was so successful that the Great Western extended its use to all its main lines, so that by 1939 it had equipped 3,250 locomotives and 2,850 track miles, contributing greatly to that company's excellent and enviable safety record.

The Great Western was by no means the only pre-Grouping (pre-1923) railway company interested in what became known as Automatic Train Control (ATC). The North Eastern Railway had a mechanical appliance at Distant signals, and equipped 1,528 locomotives and 90 route miles. Among the other railways the Great Central, the Great Eastern, the London, Brighton & South Coast and the London & North Western were all conducting experiments. The Grouping of 120 separate railway companies into the 'Big Four' in 1923, resulting from the Railways Act of 1921, led to many improvements in other fields but it severely set back the advancement of ATC. Was it mere coincidence that the only one of the 'Big Four' that went ahead with a full ATC installation, the Great Western, was the only one that was relatively unaffected by the Grouping? There may be a lesson here that re-organisations delay desirable reforms, but it is significant that almost all the worthwhile experiments in ATC which were in hand on the pre-Grouping railways came to a dead stop at the end of 1922.

But why did the other railway companies not press ahead with ATC? There were plenty of accidents to help them to make up their minds, and Inspecting Officers, in their reports, continued to press for its adoption. Col Pringle was particularly active in this, and in 1920/21 chaired a committee on the subject, whose terms of reference were:

1 To enumerate the possible functions of ATC . . . and prescribe requisites which devices should fulfil.
2 To examine ATC devices under trial and recommend for further trial or for experimental installation . . .
3 To form conclusions on the adoption of ATC, in respect of all or any of its possible functions, having regard to advantages . . . and cost.

The Report, dated April 1922, ranged over the whole subject and concluded that there was a prima facie case for warning devices to be installed at Distant signals, but that it was more important to provide trip-stop control at selected Stop signals. It suggested that the railway companies should co-operate to provide standard equipment which would allow the employment of fog-signalmen at Distant signals to be dispensed with, and which would provide for three effects — Danger, Warning and Clear. The committee was unanimous in its opposition to visual cab-signalling.

Below:
The Great Western Railway and its successor the Western Region had a remarkably good safety record, thanks to Automatic Train Control, but here is one that slipped through the net. A forlorn-looking BR Standard 'Britannia' class locomotive No 70026 *Polar Star* after its derailment at Milton, near Didcot, on 20 November 1955 whilst hauling an excursion from Treherbert to Paddington. The driver was not used to this type of locomotive and failed to react to ATC warnings, entering Milton loop at too high a speed. This is one example of many where new equipment is a contributory cause of accidents. British Railways (WR)

It might be thought that with such definite recommendations the railway companies would have acted promptly and equipped all main lines within a few years, leading to a considerable reduction in the number of serious accidents, but it did not happen. The upheaval and distraction of Grouping had some effect, although with only four companies instead of 120 it ought to have been somewhat easier to devise standard equipment. Probably the new 'Big Four' thought that the cost was too great in the more difficult financial conditions following World War 1 — the total cost was put at £4,660,000 to equip 24,000 distant signals, 38,000 stop signals and 23,000 locomotives. The proposals suffered from being too ambitious and wide-ranging, with their emphasis on train-stop equipment at Stop signals rather than warning equipment at Distant signals, whereas if the terms of reference and resulting recommendations had concentrated on the Distant signal, and if the other companies could have swallowed their pride and adopted the Great Western system, the cost would have been very much reduced and the future quite different. In the event the Great Western went its own way and the others did nothing. Accidents caused by drivers failing to react to adverse Distant signals continued to occur. If Col Pringle had expected his committee to achieve anything, he must have been very disappointed, but undaunted, and anxious to achieve something before he retired, he chaired another ATC committee in 1928/29. Its terms of reference this time were: 'To review the recommendations made by the ATC Committee of 1922 and to consider and report what alterations, if any, should be made in that Committee's conclusions and recommendations having regard to the developments that have taken place since that date.'

The membership of the committee was even more high-powered than before. The table at the top of this page details its eminent membership.

Only a few days after the committee had its first meeting on 1 October 1928, there was yet another accident of the type that ATC could have prevented, and which had disastrous results. It occurred at Charfield, between Gloucester and Bristol, on the West of England main line of the London Midland & Scottish Railway's Midland Division in the early hours of 13 October 1928, when the 10.00pm express and mail from Leeds to Bristol, hauled by ex-Midland Railway Class 3P 4-4-0 No 714, crashed at full speed into a goods train which was being set back into the down lie-by. The coaches of the express had wooden bodies and were gas-lit. An empty wagon train was passing on the next line at the precise moment and was involved in the crash, the wooden wagons helping to feed the fire which broke out. Fifteen lives were lost. It was a dramatic and spectacular accident which must have done much to concentrate the minds of the committee, whose eventual recommendations, published in 1930, proposed both 'Direct' and 'Indirect' methods of increasing security. This time the committee made a firm recommendation in favour of the Great Western fixed-ramp system at Distant signals, and whilst it proposed increased security at Stop signals this was rather a secondary consideration. The Distant signal had won the day.

The 'Indirect' methods proposed were designed to assist enginemen 'to carry out their duties of observation of, and obedience to, signals. To improve sighting facilities from the cab by designing and constructing locomotives and glasses so that steam and smoke may be cleared from the

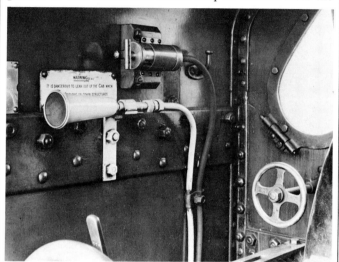

line of vision; and by positioning signals so that having regard to their background, height, etc, they will most readily come into line with the view obtainable from the engine cab. To increase the illuminative and penetrative power of signal lights themselves'.

It was also proposed that Block Signalling controls of the type referred to in Chapter 6 should be extended on 'important traffic roads'. Finally, there was mention of a recently-developed inductive control system (known as the Hudd system) which impressed the committee sufficiently for it to persuade the Southern Railway to give the necessary facilities for its first trial under working conditions at Byfleet.

What were the results of the second Pringle Committee? The Great Western, pleased that the Report had endorsed its ATC system so emphatically, went ahead and expanded its use over all its main lines, aided by Government Guaranteed Loan Schemes, but it refused to have much to do with colour-light signals. The London, Midland & Scottish Railway held perfunctory trials of the Hudd system at Millers Dale, but put its faith in 'Indirect'

Left:
The Strowger-Hudd inductive control system in the driving cab. The warning hooter sounded a short or continuous blast depending on whether the signal was in the Clear position, or against the driver. Next to the hooter can be seen the device by which the driver could stop the hooter sounding, and release the brake if appropriate. Ian Allan Library

Below left:
Strowger-Hudd warning magnets in experimental use in 1931. They operated the warning hooter in the engine cab, and applied the brakes throughout the train if the signal was at Caution. Ian Allan Library

Below:
Northallerton signalbox, seen in 1984. It houses one of the first electrical-relay interlocking systems, and came into operation on the day that World War 2 broke out — 3 September 1939. L. Abram

methods, by embarking, among other things, on a major programme to replace semaphore Distant signals with electrically-lit colour-light signals. The Southern Railway went in extensively for multiple-aspect colour-light signalling to assist the working of its intensive and growing electrified suburban and main line services. The London & North Eastern Railway took little action on the recommendations in the Report, but was very progressive in one sphere. In the 1930s it introduced an electrical relay interlocking system on the main line between York and Northallerton, complete with continuous track-circuiting, route-setting switches on a panel instead of cumbersome signal levers, and automatic colour-light signals. ATC was virtually ignored by all the railway companies except the Great Western, despite the high-powered signatories of the recommendations of the ATC Committee Report, and despite the Charfield accident, and one cannot escape the feeling that the railway companies had merely taken part in the committee for the sake of appearances, and never had any real intention of actually doing anything. Financially the railways were in difficulties, and there was little money to spare for investment of a type whose effects could not easily be measured by accountants. The 1921 Railways Act had fixed at about £50 million the standard net revenue which Parliament had decided was a fair remuneration to railway share-holders. The actual results for 1929 were £45 million, for 1930 they were £38 million and for 1931 £33 million. The lowest point was reached in 1932 when net revenue was only £26 million, in the depths of the trade depression, and there was only a slow improvement in succeeding years to £38 million in 1937. The LNER was hit particularly hard by the depression because it depended so much on heavy industries for its business. In such circumstances it is not difficult to imagine railway boards of management looking bleakly on proposals for additional investment in safety, given the generally high standards which already existed.

As already explained, except on the GWR only very small-scale experiments and trials were embarked on, a

situation which was aggravated by the doubts and indecision which surrounded the subject and which may be summarised as:

1 Which ought to have first priority for investment, Distant signals or Stop signals?
2 What indications should ATC give to the driver at the Distant signal?
3 Should ATC be installed at colour-light signals?
4 How should double-yellow colour-light signals be dealt with?
5 How should ATC, conversion of semaphore signals to colour-light or intensified light, and installation of Block Controls in signalboxes, rank with each other for priority of treatment for investment?

There was a further factor. Conversion to colour-light signalling brought not only increased safety but also other benefits. Maintenance costs were reduced, the need to change oil-lamps weekly was avoided, and the signals could be operated normally during fog because of their penetrating beam, so avoiding the need for fog-signalmen. Given all this, plus the increase in safety which was thought to follow from the more visually-arresting colour-light signal, especially at night and during poor visibility, it can be seen how easily a strong case could be made out for the extension of colour-light signalling rather than the adoption of ATC, when there was not sufficient money available for both. Much faith was put in colour-light signalling on its own as an increased safety factor. How much that faith was justified is impossible to judge; it can only be pointed out that colour-light distants were involved in some of the worst accidents in railway history:

Bourne End	30 September 1945	43 killed
Harrow and Wealdstone	8 October 1952	112 killed
St Johns, Lewisham	4 December 1957	90 killed

There were others, but supporters of colour-light signals could argue that there might have been even more if semaphore signals had not been converted to colour-light, and that intensive electrified suburban services could not have been operated without multiple-aspect colour-light signalling. Both schools of thought were correct; colour-light signalling and ATC are complementary, not competitive. It is interesting to note that the railways considered it safe to discontinue the use of fog-signalmen at colour-light Distant signals (despite some evidence to the contrary), yet persisted with their employment at the relatively safer semaphore Distant signal equipped with ATC right up to the 1980s.

By the outbreak of World War 2, enthusiasm for train-stops at selected Stop signals had completely evaporated and the various concepts of ATC were merging in favour of warning control at the Distant signal. The LMSR had been slowly developing the Hudd system and in 1935 it decided to equip the former London, Tilbury & Southend line between Campbell Road Junction (Bow) and Shoeburyness, because of its proneness to fog. By the outbreak of war the experimental work was approaching completion but the system was still not in full use. Overall, very slow progress had been made with ATC in the nine years since the Report of the second Pringle Committee. On the LNER almost nothing had been done, although that company had been stung into belated action by the crash at Castlecary on the Glasgow-Edinburgh main line on 10 December 1937 (see Appendix for details of this and other collisions not described in the text), and had started making preparations for trials of Hudd apparatus on that line. All work ceased during the war, and after it there were

more urgent matters to concern railway boards of management. The railway system had been severely overworked and under-maintained during the war, and with the return of a Labour Government in the summer of 1945 there was the prospect of Nationalisation.

The collision at Ecclefechan on 23 July 1945 and the derailment at Bourne End on 30 September 1945 focussed attention on the subject yet again. Once more the Inspecting Officer, Lt-Col Sir Alan Mount, made the now standard plea for ATC. Once more it fell on deaf ears, indeed it seemed that the railways had virtually set their face against ATC when they replied that:

'apart from the question of finance, the general installation of ATC, even of the warning type, on main lines where this does not already exist, would occupy a considerable time and employ a large number of skilled men. The supply of such staff is strictly limited, and its employment on this installation would therefore necessarily delay the execution of other work such as the modernisation of signalling, the extension of track circuiting and other similar works.'

This reply was in some ways understandable. The railway companies could not get enough staff of the right calibre, new equipment was in short supply, and, as always, there wasn't enough money. It was all the railways could do just to keep abreast of their very heavy freight traffic. ATC must necessarily have been well down their list of priorities, except of course on the Great Western, who must have been grateful for their prewar foresight. On a minor note, however, the Hudd system on the London Tilbury & Southend line had proved its reliability and was approved by the Minister of Transport in 1947.

And so matters stood when the four main line companies were nationalised on 1 January 1948 and the Railway Executive was formed. This new body initially took a more positive view, aided by reduced financial worries and the early optimism of the new undertaking. In the next five years there were studies, experiments and trials to decide the final form that ATC should take on British Railways. At first the Great Western system was favoured but it was thought to have problems if adopted in other parts of the country, especially on electrified lines, and a preference emerged for a modified Hudd system. However, it proved very difficult to embody the modifications desired and the years slipped by. Progress was disappointingly slow and it was not until August 1952 that the drawings were ready for what was hoped would be the final prototype design. The first set of equipment was fitted to a locomotive and put into service on 17 October 1952, nine days after the Harrow & Wealdstone disaster. The appalling nature of that accident obviously impressed itself upon the Railway Executive, which announced almost at once that as soon as the equipment was proved to be satisfactory, it would embark upon a five-year plan to equip 1,332 miles of the most important main lines, followed by a longer term plan to equip a further 4,000 route miles, in addition to the 1,400 route miles already equipped. This was indeed a comprehensive plan. Unfortunately, the satisfactory proving of equipment again took longer than expected, and the system was not finally approved until November 1956, four

Right:
The pile of wreckage after the worst peace-time accident in British railway history — the high-speed collision of three passenger trains at Harrow & Wealdstone station on 8 October 1952 which left 112 people dead, and which could have been prevented by Automatic Train Control. Ian Allan Library

years later, and 26 years after the second Pringle Committee Report. An allocation of £20 million was included in the British Transport Commission Plan for the Modernisation and Re-equipment of British Railways, issued in 1955.

Progress was still not very rapid — the original plans of 1953 had envisaged over 6,700 route miles being equipped, but because of delays in the supply of equipment it was 1958 before work got under way. It had originally been planned to equip 568 route miles by the end of 1959, but this was not to be achieved. The awful disasters of Harrow (1952) and St Johns (1957) might have been expected to provide an incentive to quicker progress, but the railways were gradually becoming even safer in other ways, and they could point with pride to the years 1949, 1954 and 1956 in which no passenger had been killed in a train accident. Against the background of such a superb safety record, Harrow and St Johns might have been thought of as aberrations — tragic enough but not indicative of widespread shortcomings in British Railways' safety defences. However, during the 1960s, work on the installation of ATC, now known as the Automatic Warning System (AWS), went ahead rapidly, aided by a number of large-scale re-resignalling schemes, so that by the end of 1972 nearly 3,000 route miles had been equipped with British Railways standard AWS. Progress continued to be made throughout the 1970s, and by the end of 1985 a total of 6,313 route miles had been equipped, which included the replacement of all the former Great Western equipment in order to achieve standardisation. So, almost exactly a hundred years after the trials of Kempe & Rowell's patent apparatus at Wimbledon, the programme to equip all important lines on British Railways is approaching completion, but as long as there are important lines without AWS, safety will be at risk, as was demonstrated so spectacularly at Eccles.

It might be instructive to look back to Lt-Col G. R. S. Wilson's Report on the Harrow accident to see what reservations and doubts he might have had, and whether these have been borne out in practice. No doubt Lt-Col Wilson was anxious not to dilute the force of his recommendations by expressing doubts, or suggesting variations, but the following comments are of interest:

'there should be no objection to the same footplate indication for the caution and danger indications of a multi-aspect signal, bearing in mind that ATC must always be regarded as an auxiliary to personal observation of the signals, and not as a substitute for it . . . I consider that, from the safety point of view, there is no need for differentiation on the footplate between the Yellow and Double Yellow indications at a four-aspect signal.'

Perhaps he had the Southern Region particularly in mind. It had followed the tradition of its predecessor, the Southern Railway, in extending the use of multiple-aspect colour-light signalling, which it believed yielded more benefit in terms of safety than other forms of investment, and which had contributed greatly to the Southern's excellent safety record. Coupled with the greatly improved forward view which the driver has from an electric multiple-unit train compared with a steam locomotive, the Southern considered AWS to be lower on the scale of priorities than continuous track-circuiting and colour-light signalling, a view which was also held by some operators outside the Southern. Despite Lt-Col Wilson's remarks, the Southern had misgivings about a warning system which had the same effect at signals showing two yellows, one yellow or red, as much of their intensive suburban service was worked on signals showing one or two yellows — inevitable with the close running of trains — and they feared that continuous acknowledgement of AWS warnings by the driver might lead to subconscious automatic cancellation and eventual disaster, as was to be demonstrated at Wembley on 11 October 1984, when an electric multiple-unit train from Euston to Bletchley ran past a Danger signal and collided with a Freightliner train which was just leaving Willesden sidings.

Progress in installing the Automatic Warning System on the Southern Region was very slow. In addition to the doubts which the Southern had about the standard British Railways AWS there was the technical difficulty of

Above left:
Removing GWR Automatic Train Control installations on the North Warwick line between Birmingham Moor Street and Stratford-upon-Avon in 1979, prior to their replacement by standard BR AWS equipment. This photograph was taken at Stratford-upon-Avon. British Rail (LMR)

Above:
The missing link — the warning magnet now installed on the approach to Eccles Distant signal. Had it been there on 4 December 1984 the collision would almost certainly not have happened. Author

installing it on lines electrified on the conductor rail system, which was not overcome until 1963. Even then little progress was made. To overcome the fears about repetitive cancellation, work was started on a more advanced system which gave individual signal aspects in the driving cab and required the driver to acknowledge each indication by a separate and distinct action, but the project was beset by technical difficulties and by 1973 no fully proven system was available, whilst the cost was estimated to be nearly three times that of the standard British Railways system. By this time there was pressure from all sides for the Southern to install AWS without further delay, and development work on the Southern's own AWS finally came to a halt. A belated start was then made in equipping the electrified lines with the British Railways standard AWS, after which fairly rapid progress was made, although the work is not expected to be complete until 1988/89.

The gap in the Southern's safety defences was cruelly exposed on the Brighton main line just before midnight on 19 December 1978 between Hassocks and Preston Park when the 21.50 electric multiple-unit train from London Victoria to Brighton, which was standing at a signal, was run into at almost full speed by a similar train, the 21.40 Victoria-Littlehampton. Three people were killed, including the driver of the 21.40. The Inspecting Officer, Maj Rose, in his Report, stated that if the signals had been provided with AWS, he thought the accident would not have occurred. He also commented that:

'after years of well-intentioned although, in the end, fruitless delay, during which time the Southern Region has been less well protected against the possibility of serious rear-end collisions than other Regions, there is now a firm and realistic programme for bringing the Region up to standard. It is to be hoped that neither technical difficulty nor financial stringency will be allowed to stand in the way of the successful completion of the programme within the planned timescale.'

The urgent need to complete the programme was emphasised by further collisions on the Southern, which would almost certainly have been prevented by AWS. Among them were:

1 At Parks Bridge Junction near Lewisham on 18 August 1981 the 07.49 Charing Cross-Bromley North passed a signal at Danger and came into contact with the rear of the 06.18 Dover-Cannon Street, which was crossing from the Up Fast line to the Up Slow line in front of it. Fortunately there were no injuries but a few seconds the wrong way could have resulted in tragedy.
2 At Bromley Junction on 13 November 1981 the 08.22 West Croydon-London Bridge passed a signal at Danger and came into side-long collision with the 08.23 Beckenham-Victoria. Fortunately again, there were no serious injuries.
3 At East Croydon on 16 January 1982 the 23.18 empty van train from Brighton to London Bridge, which was standing in platform 1, was run into in the rear at about 30mph by an Engineer's works train, whose driver had passed the protecting signal at Danger. Damage was estimated to be in excess of £¾ million.

Only systems such as AWS can provide a safeguard against a driver's error or inattention. Very soon now, when the installation of AWS on selected routes has been completed, Col Pringle and all the other Inspecting Officers who have pressed for so long and so hard for ATC and later for AWS (together with those Railway Officers who had faith in it) against what must often have seemed intransigent and obstructive railway managements, will have been vindicated. Only the Great Western emerges from this story with credit. The other railway companies and their successors have since 1923 almost consistently dragged their feet. Yet during the hundred years that this story has covered, the art of signalling has progressed from the simple and rudimentary to the most technically advanced, with computers and solid-state interlocking; in fact signal engineering is in the vanguard of progress, and a shining example of the application of scientific discovery and knowledge to railways. So what is the reason for this apparent paradox? It is perhaps to be found in the membership of Pringle's committees, which consisted of a Civil Engineer, a Signalling Engineer, a Locomotive Engineer and an Operating Superintendent.

With so many departments concerned there was ample scope for delay, vacillation and lack of whole-hearted commitment. If Automatic Train Control had been considered to be an integral part of the signalling system and directly and totally the responsibility of the Signal Engineer, it is surely impossible to believe that it would have taken more than 100 years to equip the railways with this simple safeguard. Have Signal Engineers assumed that their responsibilities finish at the lens of the colour-light signal or the arm of the semaphore signal, without ensuring that the message those signals give is correctly received, interpreted and acted upon by the driver? If so, many people would think that those responsibilities ought to be extended and that they should not end until the signal's instruction is correctly obeyed by the driver. After all, the

Signal Engineer has provided the signalman with every conceivable safeguard to ensure that he operates his signals safely; why has the driver, who must obey those signals correctly if safety is to be achieved, been excluded from the process?

The present Automatic Warning System is a quite simple concept, designed for Absolute Block signalling with separate Distant and Stop signals. Its application to multiple-aspect signals capable of displaying two yellows, one yellow and red is not entirely satisfactory, as we have seen, because the same warning indications are given if the signal is showing anything other than green. Lt-Col Wilson in his comments on the Harrow crash (1952) thought there was no objection to it, possibly on the realistic grounds that it was better to have reasonable protection now rather than perfection at some unknown date in the future. In view of the lack of progress up to that date he can hardly be criticised for his view. The Southern saw difficulties, and their fears have not been entirely groundless. The collision at Wembley in 1984 was only one example of several cases where crashes have occurred despite all modern safeguards including AWS being provided. On 22 July 1981 the 16.10 High Speed Train (HST) from Bristol to Paddington passed a signal at Danger and collided with a parcels train which was standing at the next signal near Hayes & Harlington. Fortunately the driver had reacted to the AWS warning at the red signal and had managed to reduce his speed from 100mph to 15/20mph at the time of the collision, but the warnings which were given at the two previous signals were ineffective. There were no serious injuries but all the components of a major disaster were there. All high speed trains carry a driver and co-driver when travelling at speeds over 100mph but the extra driver was of no avail in this case. On 31 May 1985, near Battersea Park, the 09.20 'Gatwick Express' ran into the back of the 08.51 East Grinstead-Victoria. At the Public Inquiry it was stated that the driver of the train from Gatwick had passed a succession of double-yellow and yellow signals, properly cancelling the AWS warning in each case, but when he finally received the same warning sound at the Red signal protecting the East Grinstead train he failed to notice the difference in the signal.

The weakness of the AWS might be thought to be the ability of the driver to over ride the automatic application of the brake at a Caution signal. Without that ability, Wembley and the other collisions just mentioned would not have happened, so is it feasible to remove that ability? Unfortunately it is not, because the result would be widespread disruption and delay to the train service every day. Trains frequently run on successive double-yellow Caution signals with little reduction in speed, and often the next signal in front of a driver may change to Proceed after he has received a Caution at the previous signals. It would be intolerable for trains to be brought to a stand every time

Above right & right:
Disaster on the Southern Region. Scenes at Sweethill Bridge on the Brighton main line on 20 December 1978 after the previous evening's 21.40 EMU from London Victoria to Littlehampton had run into the 21.50 EMU from Victoria to Brighton, which was standing at a signal. AWS could have prevented this.
Colin Burnham

Above:
The remains of the driving trailer belonging to unit No 7333, at the rear of the 21.50 Victoria-Brighton which was struck by the 21.40 Victoria-Littlehampton. The additional danger in the event of an accident involving vehicles with blue asbestos insulation can readily be appreciated.
Colin Burnham

Year	Location	Passenger fatalities	Speed on impact	Observations
1978	Hassocks-Preston Park (SR)	1	45/50mph	Preventable by AWS, now installed
1979	Paisley (ScR)	5	35/40mph	AWS not involved
1979	Invergowrie (ScR)	3	60mph	AWS not involved
1981	Seer Green (LMR)	3	30mph	AWS not involved
1983	Wrawby Junction (ER) (Lincs)	1	20/25mph	AWS not involved
1984	Wembley (LMR)	3	50/55mph	Preventable by improved AWS
1984	Eccles (LMR)	2	45/50mph	Preventable by AWS, now installed

in such circumstances. What is needed is a system where the automatic brake application cannot be over ridden by a thoughtless driver, in that it requires a specific choice of action by the driver depending on the precise signal aspect. Alternatively, monitoring apparatus is needed to check that a driver has correctly responded to the signal's message, and interposes if he has not. The present AWS system is showing its age and something better is going to be needed in the future, especially if speeds are to rise. To some extent the reservations of the Southern have been shown to be well-founded, but whether British Railways has either the will or the money for a better system remains to be seen, yet it seems inconceivable that the railways of Britain might enter the 21st century with a protection system which started in the 19th century.

Finally, a glance at the list of collisions at the top of this page that have resulted in the deaths of passengers in the 10 years 1976-85 may serve to show how much is owed to AWS.

Is it mere chance that the Western Region is absent, or a tribute to the foresight of its predecessor?

Less than one fatal collision, and only two passengers killed, on average each year, shows a very high safety standard indeed. One cannot say how much longer the list would have been without AWS — it is a matter of conjecture, but the very small number of fatalities in each collision is also very notable — only as many as are killed in a single car crash on the roads of this country every day of the year. We have to go back as far as 1962 to find more than 10 passenger deaths in a collision; a record of which coach designers and builders, as well as all railwaymen, can be very proud.

Because of the widespread installation of AWS there were only two collision in which passengers were killed where there was no AWS, and which AWS could have prevented, in the 10-year period 1976-85, and both locations have now been equipped. An examination of the period before AWS started to be installed (based on train accidents into which Government inquiries were held) gives an interesting comparison:

1930-37 (eight years): 13 accidents preventable by AWS. 63 fatalities.

1938-52 (15 years): 15 accidents preventable by AWS. 241 fatalities.

1976-85 (10 years): two accidents preventable by AWS. Three passengers and three staff killed.

The figures speak for themselves, although it has to be remembered that there were many collisions without fatalities, but nevertheless resulting in injuries, and in very costly damage and delay.

Appendix 1

Automatic Warning Systems, ATC, Hudd and AWS

The Great Western Railway Automatic Train Control System

Track equipment:
A fixed ramp approximately 50ft long lying in the 'four-foot' between the rails, near the Distant signal. When the signal is 'Clear' an electric current is applied to the ramp.

Locomotive equipment:
A pick-up shoe is located beneath the locomotive, which engages the ramp. When the signal is at Caution a magnetically-operated valve, normally held closed by a current from a battery on the locomotive, is opened and allows air to enter the brake pipe and apply the brakes. A siren also sounds as a warning. When the signal is 'Clear' the electric current which passes through the ramp is picked up by the shoe and holds the valve closed. It also sounds a bell.

Cab equipment:
A siren, to sound a warning.
A bell, to sound 'Clear'.
Equipment to overcome the automatic application of the brake when a Warning is received.
No visual indicator.

Later developments:
Additional electrical equipment to differentiate between two yellows and one yellow at a Distant signal. The ramp is energised with the opposite polarity and sounds both the siren and a horn at a double-yellow signal.

Below:
BR Standard AWS equipment. A permanent magnet and an electro-magnet laid in the 'four-foot'. British Railways (LMR)

Left:
Cab layout of an electric locomotive. The AWS visual indicator is to the left of the driver's windscreen. AEI

Above:
Close-up of the AWS visual indicator. Author

The Hudd Non-Contact System of Automatic Train Control

The original Strowger-Hudd system had a permanent magnet and an electro-magnet in the 'four-foot' 200ft before the Distant signal, and a combined permanent and electro-magnet at the Stop signal. On the locomotive there was a receiver, a hooter, and an acknowledgement plunger. At a Clear Distant signal a short hoot was given, at a Caution Distant signal a long hoot was given, and at a Stop signal no indication was given. At a Caution Distant signal and a Danger Stop signal there was an automatic brake application, which the driver could override with his acknowledgement plunger only at the Distant signal. There was no visual indicator in the cab.

As later developed by the LMS Railway the system was installed only at Distant signals, and worked as follows:
Track equipment:
A permanent magnet and an electro-magnet are located in the 'four-foot' at the approach to a Distant signal. When the signal is 'Clear' the electro-magnet is energised.
Locomotive equipment:
A receiver fixed underneath the locomotive reacts to the magnets on the track. When it passes over the permanent magnet it sounds a siren and applies the brake after a short delay. If the electro-magnet is energised the siren is shut off and the brake application does not take place. The driver can override the brake application, in which case a visual indicator in the cab will display a segmented disc coloured alternately black and yellow.

The British Railways standard Automatic Warning System of Train Control (AWS)

Track equipment:
A permanent magnet and an electro-magnet are installed in

the 'four-foot' about 200yd on the approach side of those signals which can display a Caution aspect.
Locomotive equipment:
A receiver is fixed underneath the locomotive and reacts to the magnets fixed in the track. If the signal is 'Clear' the electro-magnet is energised and a bell sounds in the driving cab. If the signal is not 'Clear' the electro-magnet remains not energised, a horn sounds in the driving cab and the brake is applied. The driver can stop the horn sounding and override the brake application by pressing a cancelling plunger, in which case a visual indicator in the cab will display a segmented disc coloured alternately black and yellow.

Solid-state equipment is used in the most recent builds of locomotives and multiple-units, replacing the mechanical bell and visual indicator, but the principle is unchanged.

Appendix 2

Standards which BR adopts to decide whether or not a line should be equipped with AWS

AWS is to be provided on the following:

1 Lines on which speeds of 75mph and over are allowed, with a substantial volume of express passenger trains.
2 Lines with a high density of suburban passenger trains.
3 Lines with a substantial density of passenger and freight trains, and lines scheduled to carry heavy freight trains.
4 Lines which are often foggy.
5 Short stretches of line between routes equipped under other criteria, which together form part of a through route.
6 Lines on which there is more than one train per hour in either direction between midnight and 06.00 (lines must be at least 20 miles long and speeds at least 40mph).

Condition **5** is designed to give AWS safeguards to drivers working trains on parts of different trunk routes already equipped, connected by lines which would not otherwise qualify. Condition **6** is designed to give AWS safeguards to drivers during those hours when there is most likelihood of drowsiness.

Appendix 3

Details of accidents not otherwise explained in the text

Castlecary (between Glasgow and Edinburgh LNER): 10 December 1937

In the late afternoon an Edinburgh-Glasgow express hauled by Gresley Pacific locomotive No 2744 *Grand Parade* ran past the signals at Danger at Castlecary during a snowfall, and collided at almost full speed with a Dundee-Glasgow express which had come to an emergency stop a little way beyond the signalbox. Although there was some dispute about the position of the Distant signal arm, Automatic Train Control would have prevented the accident if the Distant signal had been properly in the Caution position. 35 passengers were killed.

Ecclefechan (near Gretna LMSR): 23 July 1945

The 1.0pm express from Glasgow to Euston, hauled by Stanier Pacific locomotive No 6231 *Duchess of Atholl*, crashed sidelong at 60/65mph into a freight train which was setting back into the refuge siding at Ecclefechan. The driver had run past the Outer and Inner Home signals at Danger. The driver and fireman were both killed but fortunately there were no passenger fatalities. All the signals concerned were upper-quadrant semaphores.

Bourne End (near Berkhamsted LMSR): 30 September 1945

Engineering work was in progress on the Fast line and Up trains were being diverted to the Slow line through a 20mph crossover at Bourne End. The 8.20pm sleeping car express from Perth to Euston, hauled by 'Royal Scot' 4-6-0 locomotive No 6157 *The Royal Artilleryman*, became derailed when passing through the crossover at a speed of about 50/60mph. The Distant signal was a colour-light showing two yellows which meant: 'Pass next signal at restricted speed, and the points may be set through the speed-restricted crossover'. The speed of the train was not reduced in time, but Automatic Train Control might have alerted the driver and prevented the accident. 43 people were killed.

Harrow & Wealdstone (LMSR): 8 October 1952

The 8.15pm sleeping car express from Perth to Euston (the same train as at Bourne End above), hauled by Stanier Pacific No 46242 *City of Glasgow* ran past the colour-light Distant signal at Caution and the Outer and Inner Home signals at Danger and crashed at 50/60mph into the 7.31am local passenger train from Tring to Euston which was standing in the station at Harrow. Almost immediately a double-headed express, the 8.0am from Euston to Liverpool and Manchester crashed into the wreckage at about 60mph. The result was devastating and 112 people were killed, a death roll exceeded only once by the double collision at

Quintinshill near Gretna on 22 May 1915 in which 227 people were killed. Automatic Train Control would almost certainly have prevented the Harrow crash.

Lewisham St John's (Southern Region): 4 December 1957

In foggy weather the 4.56pm express from Cannon Street to Folkestone and Ramsgate hauled by a 'Battle of Britain' class Pacific locomotive No 34066 *Spitfire* ran past a colour-light signal at Red, preceded by two Caution colour-light signals showing respectively two yellows and one yellow, and crashed into the rear of the 5.18pm electric multiple-unit train from Charing Cross to Hayes which was standing at a signal at Parks Bridge Junction. The effects of the collision brought down on to the wreckage the 350ton girder bridge carrying the Nunhead loop-line. 90 people

Left:
**Bourne End (LMS)
30 September 1945.** 'Royal
Scot' class 4-6-0 No 6157 *The
Royal Artilleryman* is being
prepared for re-railing after
plunging down an
embankment. It had
attempted to negotiate a
crossover at too high a
speed. C. R. L. Coles

Below:
**The ultimate horror. Harrow
& Wealdstone station on the
morning of 8 October 1952.**
The newly-rebuilt Pacific
No 46202 *Princess Anne* (the
former 'Turbomotive') lies
across a heap of wreckage in
Britain's worst-ever peace-
time crash. Ian Allan Library

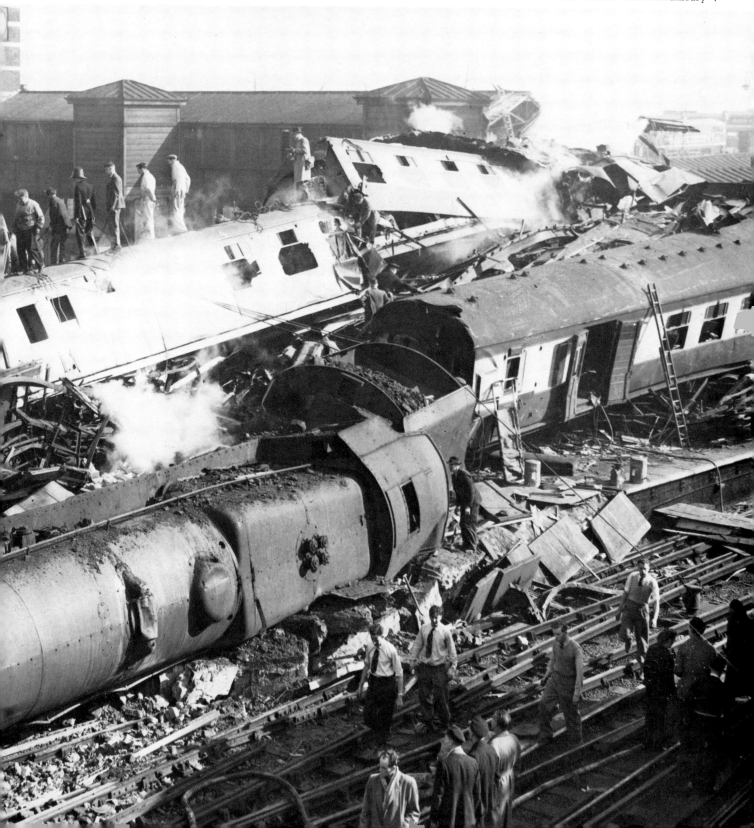

were killed. This accident would almost certainly have been prevented by automatic warning signalling.

Between Hassocks and Preston Park (Southern Region): 19 December 1978

The 21.50 12-car electric multiple-unit train from London Victoria to Brighton had been standing at a Red signal for two or three minutes just north of Patcham Tunnel when it was run into in the rear by the 21.40 Victoria to Littlehampton 8-car electric multiple-unit travelling at 45/50mph. The time was 23.22. One passenger and two railwaymen, including the driver of the 21.40, lost their lives. The second train had passed a Caution colour-light signal 1½ miles away, but there was no light in the next

Right:
The scene of the accident at Lewisham St Johns, showing the collapsed girders which were brought down by the effects of the collision, when the tender of No 34066 and the leading coach of the 4.56pm Cannon Street-Ramsgate struck and dislodged a steel column supporting them. The girders collapsed on to the front coaches of the Ramsgate train, causing many deaths. British Railways (SR)

Above right:
The bridge at Lewisham St Johns (SR) which collapsed on the wreckage of the two trains involved in the collision on 4 December 1957. Ian Allan Library

Below:
A view of the flyover at Lewisham St Johns on 12 December 1957 after the damaged section of the flyover had been removed, with the tracks beneath once again open for traffic. British Rail (SR)

signal, ¾-mile away, which should have been showing Red, protecting the stationary train. In modern colour-light installations the failure of a light in one signal will automatically switch to Danger the next signal in rear, but the signalling on the Brighton line dated from 1932 and was not so equipped, nor was AWS provided which would have operated correctly and warned the driver even if the signal light were out. The signalling has since been modernised under the Brighton line resignalling scheme, and AWS has been provided.

Wembley (London Midland Region): 11 October 1984

The 17.54 electric multiple-unit train from Euston to Bletchley, after passing several colour-light signals showing one or two yellows, ran past one at Red and collided at about 60mph with a Freightliner train which was just leaving Willesden sidings. This route is equipped with multiple-aspect colour-light signalling, continuous track circuiting and automatic warning signalling. The Inspecting Officer, Maj C. F. Rose, concluded that: 'It is entirely possible that [the driver] allowed his mind to wander or otherwise lost concentration, and cancelled the AWS warnings . . . without realising what he was doing. On the other hand, a distinguished panel of medical specialists, having examined [the driver] and studied all the available evidence, have concluded that, on the balance of probabilities [the driver's] behaviour was due to a rare but well recognised medical condition . . ., I believe he should be given the benefit of any doubt. But whatever the cause, the BR AWS was ineffective in preventing the collision.'

2 Protecting the Stranded Train

The date was 22 October 1979. The weather was quite reasonable for the time of year but on board the 08.44 passenger train from Glasgow to Dundee things were not going well. By the time the train passed Longforgan signalbox, about six miles short of its destination, it was already 25 minutes late due to mechanical difficulties with the diesel locomotive, No 25083. Power had been lost intermittently on the journey but after the driver had reset and isolated the earth fault switch he found he could obtain power satisfactorily, and a fitter at Perth said that it would be in order for the train to continue to Dundee.

After leaving Perth the train made the normal station stops at Errol and Invergowrie, but on restarting from the latter something seemed to be holding the train. The driver stopped just beyond the platform and examined the locomotive. The brakes appeared to be binding on the leading bogie and as he could not free them he decided to continue the journey, hoping to be able to reach Dundee, only three miles away. However, when he had travelled only a few hundred yards one of the traction motors was seen to be on fire, so the train was stopped again. It was then standing on the curve along the bank of the Firth of Tay, with five coaches. The engine had been shut down and after the usual sounds of the journey everything was quiet and

still, almost eerily so, with the silence punctuated only by the cries of wheeling gulls. The passengers may have felt a slight irritation at the further delay but they surely didn't feel vulnerable sitting there waiting.

Suddenly in the distance behind them could be heard the deep throb of a Class 47 locomotive being worked hard with the roar of its engine becoming ever more insistent. The guard and secondman of the 08.44 looked on horrified and helplessly as the 09.35 express from Glasgow to Aberdeen burst into view round the curve and rushed on unchecked towards them. Seconds later it hurtled into an appalling collision with their own train.

The force of the impact threw the last two coaches of the standing train over the sea wall on to the muddy foreshore, killing both occupants of the last coach. The cab of the Class 47 was completely crushed and both the driver and secondman were killed. One other passenger was fatally injured. It was fortunate that the 08.44 was not heavily loaded or the death toll would inevitably have been greater. It was also fortunate that no train was approaching on the opposite line. Nevertheless 51 people had to be taken to hospital, where 13 were detained, including four with serious injuries.

The guard and secondman of the 08.44 were astonished

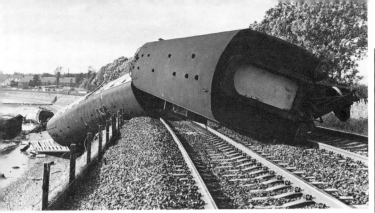

when the second train approached. How could it be? The signalling should surely have prevented it and safeguarded their train. They must have felt much as the crew of the Up Scotch sleeper felt when their train stood short of steam just north of Ais Gill summit, near Kirkby Stephen, on the night of 1 September 1913 and they heard the ominous sound of another Up Scotch express rapidly bearing down on them after it had overrun the Danger signals at Mallerstang. Or similarly at Winsford, near Crewe, in 1948 when an up express was stopped in mid-section by a soldier pulling the communication cord, and was run into by a following postal express.

Such rear-end collisions are becoming rarer, thanks to automatic warning signalling and modern electrical safety-controls in signalboxes, but at one time they were much more frequent, particularly in the 19th century. A second line of defence was therefore devised to safeguard a stranded train if a following one should pass the signalbox in rear in error. The 1883 Rule Book said:

'When a train is stopped out of course from any cause the guard must immediately go back to stop any following train, exhibiting a hand Danger signal, and place detonators on the line, one at 400 yards, one at 800 yards and two at 1,200 yards from his train.' (Railway detonators, also known as fog signals, are small devices intended to be fixed to the top of a rail in an emergency. They are exploded

This page:
Scenes of horror alongside the Firth of Tay on 22 October 1979 after the 09.35 express from Glasgow to Aberdeen had run at full speed into the 08.44 Glasgow-Dundee, which had broken down. The forces unleashed in a high-speed crash are clearly demonstrated here. Fortunately the tide was out and there were not many passengers in the stationary train. Spanphoto

27

by the wheels of a locomotive passing over them, and warn the locomen of a hazard ahead.)

Exactly 100 years later the Rules said much the same but in rather more words. And of course telephones could be used to give earlier warning if there were any nearby. Apart from that nothing had changed much in that direction. Efforts had been concentrated on trying to ensure that a second train did not pass the signalbox in rear in error, reducing the reliance on the other, rather more archaic, forms of train protection.

But why were the arrangements for train protection by detonator ineffective at Invergowrie? The answer is that they were ineffective for the same reason that they had been ineffective so many times previously — the time factor. In principle, as soon as a train stops out of course, owing to failure or derailment for example, the guard should rush off back down the line the instant it stops, with his detonators and flags or lamp, to stop any train approaching. There shouldn't be one of course; the signalling should see to that. But in theory this procedure should be followed just in case, and based on bitter experience.

In practice however it is not like that. Recent history provides few examples where such action on a guard's part has prevented a collision, and an examination of the procedures laid down in the Rule Book shows why. The guard is told that:

'If a train is stopped by accident, failure, obstruction or other exceptional cause and any other line is obstructed, or there is reason to believe this is likely, the first duty of the traincrew is to protect such lines . . . by the quickest possible means . . . when the train comes to a stand the

driver and guard must confer . . . and ascertain whether any other line is obstructed or damaged; if it is the appropriate protection arrangements must be carried out.

Trainmen, when carrying out protection, must exhibit a hand Danger signal and must place detonators . . . on the obstructed line as follows:

1 detonator ¼ mile from the obstruction
1 detonator ½ mile from the obstruction
3 detonators 1 mile from the obstruction (1¼ miles where permissible speed is 100mph or above)

If, before the trainman reaches the full distance, he comes to a signalbox or telephone, he must inform the signalman of the circumstances.'

It can be seen from this extract from the Rule Book that the traincrew's first concern is to see if *any other line* is obstructed. This is exactly as it should be because whilst their own train is protected by the signalling system, an accidental obstruction of an adjoining line may not be so protected and there would be nothing to prevent another train on such a line from running into the wreckage. But in order to find out if any other line is obstructed the guard must walk along the train to see the driver, who should be walking back to meet the guard. If they find that no other line is obstructed (the normal result in the case of the commonest stoppage, engine failure) the urgency of the situation is reduced and they then confer to decide how the failure is to be dealt with. In some cases the driver is likely to say that he expects to be able to rectify the defect within a few minutes, therefore there is no point in the guard setting off to protect his train. He would not have time to get very far before the train was ready to depart and it would only cause additional delay. If the driver is unable to rectify the defect, then the guard will set off to protect his train, and possibly also to seek assistance if it is more effective for him to do so in rear of his train rather than by the driver walking forward.

It can be seen, therefore, how time races by before the guard's protection in rear becomes effective. Possibly 10 minutes to walk down the train, confer with the driver, and return. Another 10 minutes to get at least half a mile from his train in order to give the driver of a wrongly approaching train a reasonable chance of stopping before reaching the stranded train. It is quite likely that if an error has occurred somewhere the second train will be on the scene in less than 20 minutes. Only a few minutes separated the two trains in the Invergowrie collision, and the guard of the stranded train had not even got beyond the rear of his own train. Beyond 20 minutes other safety precautions come into play. The signalmen would have become alert to the possibility of there being something wrong in the section. All trains would be stopped and the driver of the first train in the opposite direction would be told by the signalman to take his train forward cautiously, so that if his line was obstructed he would be able to stop in time.

This procedure would eventually have taken place in the section between the signalboxes at Buckingham Junction (Dundee) and Longforgan, but before it was due to be applied the fatal error had been made. However, before examining the circumstances of that fatal error, it may be appropriate to examine the safeguards which have been devised over the years to make the signalling system more and more foolproof. Let us consider the sort of errors that might occur.

1 *By the driver missing the signals at the signalbox in rear and proceeding into the forward section towards the stranded train at full speed.*
The Automatic Warning System (AWS) was devised to help drivers to observe signals, as explained in the

Above:
A LNER block instrument, made by Tyer & Co.
1 **Repeater indicator, worked by the signalman at the next signalbox beyond. The inscription 'Train on Line' means the same as 'Train in Section'.**
2 **Indicator worked by this signalman, by rotating handle (4).**
3 **The wheel of the Welwyn Control.**
4 **Rotating handle, for placing the block indicator needle in different positions.**
5 **'Tapper', for sending bell signals to the next signalman.**
6 **Signal indication repeater, for a colour-light signal out of sight of the signalman.**
7 **Signal arm repeater, for a semaphore signal out of sight of the signalman. He must observe the repeater each time he moves the signal lever to ensure that the signal arm obeys the lever.**
British Railways (LMR)

previous chapter. It had already been installed at the Longforgan Distant signal, which is a colour-light.

2 *By the signalman making an error and thinking that a train had already passed clear of the forward section whilst in reality it was still there; then clearing all his signals for a second train.*
The Absolute Block signalling system, as installed between Longforgan and Buckingham Junction signalboxes, is based on the use of block telegraph instruments and bells for passing messages between adjacent signalmen. It is operated in accordance with the Absolute Block regulations, as follows:

Before clearing his signals for a train the signalman must send the appropriate 'is line clear?' bell signal to the

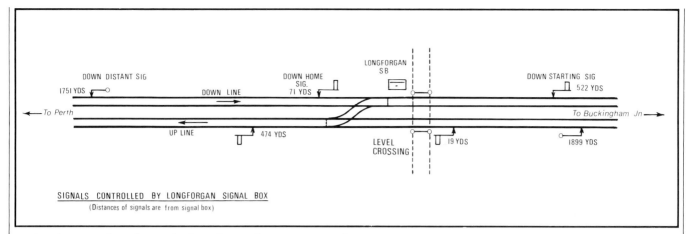

SIGNALS CONTROLLED BY LONGFORGAN SIGNAL BOX
(Distances of signals are from signal box)

signalman at the other end of the forward section. If the line *is* clear the second signalman must repeat the bell signal back to the first signalman and place the telegraph needle on his block instrument to the 'line clear' position. This 'line clear' indication is repeated on a duplicate instrument in the first signalbox and is the authority to the first signalman to clear his signals. As the train passes the first signalbox the signalman there must send the bell signal 'train entering section'. The second signalman then moves the needle on his block instrument to 'train in section'. When the train passes the second signalbox the signalman there sends back the bell signal 'train out of section' and puts the needle to its normal position. The way is now clear for another train.

The actual Absolute Block regulation is necessarily rather more wordy than that, but the above is, in essence, what happens. Provided the signalmen carry out the procedures correctly and are alert, it is absolutely safe, as has been proved times without number over a century or more, but it puts a premium on human nature, and occasionally errors occur. Such errors by their very nature are potentially calamitous and Signal Engineers have

devised various safeguards over the years, sometimes used separately and sometimes in conjunction with each other, depending on the importance of the signalbox and the density of traffic. The safeguards installed between Longforgan signalbox and Buckingham Junction signalbox at the time of the accident were:

1 The Starting signal at Longforgan was electrically locked at Danger and could not be cleared unless the signalman at Buckingham Junction had placed his block instrument to 'line clear'. Once a line-clear release had been obtained, and the signal lever had been pulled in order to clear the signal, and had then been replaced to return the signal to Danger after the train had passed, the signal could not again be cleared until a new line-clear release had been given.

Below:
Longforgan signalbox in September 1986. Class 26 diesel No 26034 running light has just passed the Down Home signal on its way from Perth to Dundee. Author

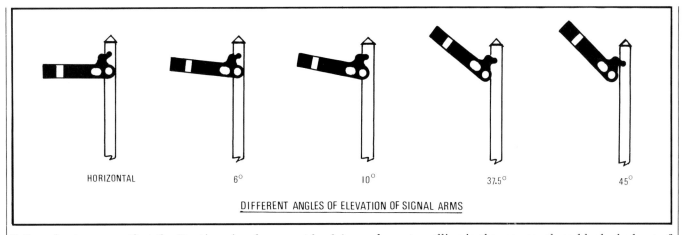

HORIZONTAL   6°   10°   37.5°   45°

2 In order to ensure that the Starting signal was put back to Danger after each train and became electrically locked, a mechanical interlock (known as sequential locking) was provided which locked the Home signal at Danger until the Starting signal lever was replaced.

3 The Home Signal at Longforgan was provided with an electrical contact which prevented the signalman there from placing his block indicator to 'line clear' unless the signal was at Danger.

This combination of line-clear release on the Starting signal, sequential locking and electrical controls required that all the signals at Longforgan were replaced to Danger and that a fresh line-clear release was obtained, before a second train could be allowed to proceed.

There was a further safeguard. Once the block instrument at Buckingham Junction had been placed to 'train in section', it could not be turned to another position until the train had arrived there and had operated an electrical circuit on the track (known as a track circuit), thus effectively preventing a second train from being allowed to come before the first one had cleared the section. (This is known as Welwyn Control.)

With all those safeguards installed it is obvious that something very unusual happened at Longforgan on the day in question. The signalman was operating his equipment correctly, and all his signals were at Danger protecting the 08.44 Glasgow-Dundee, which was in the section ahead, when the following train approached about 10 minutes later. The driver of that train, the 09.35 Glasgow-Aberdeen, will have received an AWS warning at the Distant signal, and he responded correctly, bringing his train nearly to a stand at the Home signal before the signalman cleared it to allow the train to draw down towards the Starting signal 500 yards away in order to await the clearance of the previous train and the acceptance of this one by the signalman at Buckingham Junction. What went wrong then is not clear, because both the driver and secondman were killed and vital evidence is unobtainable. According to the Rule Book the train should have drawn slowly past the Home signal, and as it approached the signalbox the driver should have been watching to see if the signalman wanted him to stop there to give him a message (about a need to travel cautiously in the section ahead for example). If there was no such indication from the signalman the driver should have continued to draw forward slowly, taking his train over the level crossing and stopping just beyond it so that the guard could go to the signalbox to remind the signalman that the train was standing there. He should not have drawn down to the Starting signal.

What actually happened, according to the evidence of the signalman and the guard, followed the instructions in the Rule Book very closely, except for the last fatal act. The guard was travelling in the rear coach and he looked out of his near-side window as the train was just approaching Longforgan signalbox at walking pace. He saw the Home signal move to the Clear position, after which the train continued slowly past the signal and over the level crossing. A moment later the train started to accelerate, and when he looked out again he saw the Starting signal 30-40 yards away. It appeared to be 'half-cocked', that is to say it was not horizontal but was not giving a proper 'Off' (ie Clear) indication. He described it as a 'poor Off'. At the subsequent Department of Transport Public Inquiry he gave his impression of the extent to which the signal arm was above horizontal as he saw it, using a full-size mock-up of a signal arm. He placed it at an angle of 7.4° — hardly 'half-cock', which would require something of the order of 20/25%. In his evidence the guard said that at the time he had not really thought about whether the signal was Clear or not; he knew the driver to be a most experienced and competent man and felt that he would not have passed the signal if it had not been properly 'Off'. In retrospect he realised that the signal was certainly not giving a proper 'Off' indication and he thought that he must have assumed at the time that the signal had been cleared and returned to Danger by the signalman and that the arm had not returned properly to the horizontal position. It is a pity that the guard's evidence on this aspect was somewhat muddled because he was the only surviving witness who had a close view of the signal. Should he have taken some emergency action at the time? It is very difficult to say yes, because the guard did not see the signal when the driver was looking at it. Secondly, when he did look out he had a much less perfect view of it than the driver, and thirdly, he was entitled to rely on the driver's judgement. It is almost unknown for a guard to query a driver's judgement in such circumstances, and although the guard in retrospect thought that he must have assumed at the time that the signal *had* been cleared for the train, and had then been replaced to Danger (without the arm going correctly to horizontal) in the five seconds or so that had elapsed between the driver passing it and the guard looking out at it, such an assumption was not unreasonable either at the time or subsequently. Finally, Maj Rose, the Inspecting Officer who held the Public Inquiry, attached no blame to the guard; a conclusion from which it is difficult to dissent.

The signalman's evidence was similar to the guard's. He said he had replaced the Starting signal after the passage of the previous train, the 08.44 Glasgow-Dundee, and he saw it clearly go back correctly to Danger. The following train, the 09.35 Glasgow-Aberdeen, drew slowly past his signalbox and he thought he might have waved to the locomen. He certainly waved at the guard. As the train approached the Starting signal it started to pick up speed and went past the signal, which as far as he could see was still at Danger. He

went down on to the track and saw that from there the signal arm appeared to be slightly raised, about 4°.

It will remain for ever a mystery as to why the driver of the 09.35 went past Longforgan's Starting signal at Danger. Could the driver really have taken it for a Clear indication? As soon as the Home signal was cleared (ie moved to the Clear position) he would almost certainly have looked forward to see if the Starting signal was going to be cleared also, and it is evident that at that point he did not think that the Starting signal *was* clear, because he continued to draw forward slowly, past the signalbox and over the level crossing, and as he still did not accelerate it can be deduced that he still thought that the Starting signal was at Danger, or at least that he was undecided as to whether it was at Danger or at Clear. At this point along the line he should have stopped to allow the guard to go to the signalbox, as provided for in the Rules, but for some reason he continued to draw forward slowly. He may have thought that there was a track circuit between the Home signal and the Starting signal, which would have avoided the need for him

to stop to allow the guard to go to the signalbox. The existence of such track circuits is indicated at the signal by a white diamond plate fixed to the signal post, but because trains were so rarely stopped at Longforgan it is possible that the situation had never previously arisen for the driver. According to the evidence of both the guard and the signalman the train did not start to accelerate until it was approaching the Starting signal. Possibly the driver had looked away from the signal for some reason and then when he looked up he may have decided that the signal was supposed to be Clear. That seems to be the most likely explanation but we can never be certain. No one will ever know exactly what took place in the driving cab in those last few moments before the fatal mistake was made. Nor shall we ever know whether the driver's assistant concurred with the driver's view, but we do know from experience that a driver's assistant will rarely query his driver's actions or decisions, and there is no evidence on which we can attach any blame to him in this case.

It is fortunately quite rare for accidents to be caused by

drivers going past 'half-cocked' signals which are supposed to be at Danger. However, there was such an accident at Winwick Junction, just north of Warrington, on 11 July 1967 when a diesel multiple-unit train went past a 'half-cocked' signal of 17° at Winwick Quay signalbox and collided with a freight train, fortunately without fatalities; but with so few accidents from such a cause it is difficult to justify heavy expenditure on remedial measures. AWS-type magnets at Starting signals, or co-acting detonators, would provide reasonable safeguards but to treat all Starting signals like that would be to incur unjustifiably heavy expenditure. The 'half-cock' problem does not arise with colour-light signals, but to replace all semaphore Starting signals with colour-light signals would be a very expensive solution. Radio would also provide a possible safeguard if the equipment were sufficiently sophisticated to enable the signalman to contact the driver in the relatively short time available, yet still leave time for the driver to stop his train before colliding with the train in front — a total of only two or three minutes in the case of the Invergowrie accident. The possibility of another 'Invergowrie' will diminish as the use of radio and colour-light signalling spreads, but it will be around for a long time yet.

This accident has brought into the spotlight a number of important Rules and it would now be appropriate to have a look at them in more detail.

When is a semaphore signal properly 'Off'?
Rule C. 3.2.1. says 'arm raised or lowered 45°', whilst there is a technical tolerance which allows the arm to be anywhere between a minimum of 37½° and maximum of 65°. Where signals are a long way from signalboxes, expansion and contraction of the operating wire in hot and cold weather can make a substantial difference in the extent to which the arm moves when the signal lever is pulled. Wire adjusters are normally provided in the case of signals which are a long way from the signalbox so that the signalman can adjust the tension of the wire to compensate for the effect of temperature variations. Where the signal is out of his sight an electrical indicator, known as a 'repeater', is provided in the signalbox to show the position of the signal arm. It is usually a three-position indicator showing 'On', 'Wrong' and 'Off'. There is a 5° tolerance before 'Wrong' is shown. The signalman is required by Rule to observe the signal arm or its repeater every time he operates a lever, to make sure it responds correctly. If it does not do so, and if he is unable to rectify matters by using his wire adjuster, the signal must be treated as being defective. (At the time of the accident there was neither wire adjuster nor repeater for the Starting signal at Longforgan.)

In practice, however, the driver is presented with a wide variety of signal-arm positions, usually around 45° for signals near the signalbox but occasionally going as low as 25° or 30° for more distant ones, especially on a hot sunny morning after a cold night. What is the driver to do? The Rule Book clearly says 45°. It also clearly says that a signal imperfectly exhibited must be treated as a Danger signal, but this is where theory and practice divide. Drivers know from experience how to judge whether a signal can safely be considered to be 'Off' but there is obviously an area from 30/25° downwards where increasing doubts ought to arise in a driver's mind and where he ought to be querying the

Right:
The white diamond-shaped plate on Settle Junction's Up Starting Signal tells drivers that their trains are on a track circuit at that point and that they do not need to go to the signalbox to remind the signalman of their presence if they are stopped there by the signal being at red. Author

matter with the signalman. However, drivers do not always stop to do so, as is demonstrated perhaps by the Invergowrie accident and certainly by the Winwick Junction accident. It is too easy to assume that anything other than horizontal must have been pulled by the signalman; perhaps because that assumption is usually correct.

When the Starting signal is at danger the Home signal must not be taken 'Off' for an approaching train until the train is close to the Home signal and has been brought nearly to a stand.

This rule, of very ancient lineage (it was in the Rule Book 100 years ago), is designed to avoid a driver overlooking the danger message of the Starting signal. It is well understood by drivers and is applied day in/day out, times without number. However, to be absolutely safe it needs to be applied meticulously by the signalman so that the driver is in no doubt as to its message — you may pass the Home signal but be prepared to stop at the signalbox; the Starting signal is at Danger. Even this procedure was not absolutely safe at Longforgan on 22 October 1979, but we shall never know why. The Rule was certainly correctly applied by the signalman, but there can be an area of doubt in the application of the Rule. If the signalman comes to be in a position to clear all his signals just as the train is

Top:
Britain's worst ever railway disaster occurred at Quintinshill on the Caledonian Railway, near Gretna Green, in 1915, when 227 people were killed, mainly soldiers. The scene is partly obscured in this photograph by smoke rising from the remains of the burnt-out troop train. If the rules had been properly carried out the accident would not have happened.
British Railways (LMR)

Above:
Quintinshill 58 years later, even after all modern safeguards had been applied. Fortunately only freight trains were involved when one ran into the back of another which was standing at the Starting signal. The driver of the second train admitted dozing off after sighting the Distant signal at Caution and agreed that he must have cancelled the AWS warning before falling asleep. G. Kinghorn

approaching the signalbox what is the driver to assume? And how far away does the train have to be before the driver can be sure that the clearance of the Home signal means that the line ahead is now clear? Drivers would normally be specially alert if they were to pass a Distant signal at Caution and then see the Home signal 'Off' some distance away, but if the Home signal is cleared just as they are approaching it, it is giving one of two radically opposing messages:

1 You may pass the Home signal, and the line ahead is clear, or

2 You may pass the Home signal, but the line ahead is *not* clear;

although strictly speaking it is saying 'You may pass me but I'm saying nothing about the state of things ahead. You must look out for yourself'. Hence the need for special care, of which drivers are very well aware. It might be thought that semaphore Stop signals could only give two messages — 'Stop', and 'Go' — but as we have seen they can give a variety of messages depending on how they are operated in relation to the position of the train.

There was an accident involving the operation of the Home signal, which occurred at Kirby Cross, between Colchester and Walton-on-the-Naze on 5 April 1981, when an electric multiple-unit passed the Starting signal at Danger and collided head-on, fortunately at low speed, with an approaching train on the single line ahead. The conclusion of the Public Inquiry was that the signalman had cleared his Home signal too soon and that the driver had overlooked the Starting signal. In passing, it is interesting to note that a co-acting detonator-placer was installed at the Starting signal, but it was ineffective because it was badly worn.

The Rule Book attempts to lay down a code of practice which will enable trains to be worked safely and efficiently in all circumstances, but there are two unofficial customs which have been in widespread use for many years and they concern this particular rule. The first one is designed to help the driver to know whether the section ahead is still blocked when the Home signal is cleared just as he is approaching it. When the section ahead is not clear, the signalman will pull the lever of the Home signal quite slowly and deliberately, causing the signal arm to move slowly. Drivers seeing this understand that the section ahead is not clear, and act accordingly. The second unofficial custom is designed to assist drivers, who have been almost stopped at the Home signal, to know whether the Starting signal is 'Off' or not when it is out of sight. At such places it is often the practice for the signalman to lean out of the signalbox window and give the 'all right' hand signal to the driver, meaning: 'I have cleared the Starting signal'. If there is no hand signal, it can be taken to mean that the Starting signal is still at Danger. It was a useful practice in the days of heavy, loose-coupled trains because it enabled the driver to control his train more smoothly. These unofficial practices are only safe if everyone knows what they mean, but arms in the air can be misleading, as a tractor driver found to his cost at Catholme level crossing near Wichnor Junction, between Burton-on-Trent and Tamworth, on 15 February 1969, when he misunderstood the signalman's hand signal not to cross the line and drove his tractor and trailer into the path of a three-car diesel multiple-unit which was approaching at 60mph.

When a train is brought to a stand owing to a Stop signal being at Danger, a member of the traincrew must go to the signalbox to remind the signalman of the presence of the train.

This is another link with the early days of railways. It does not apply if the train is standing on a track circuit (indicated by a white diamond plate on the signal post) but it did apply at Longforgan because there was no track circuit between the Home signal and the Starting signal. The train should have been stopped just beyond the level crossing to allow the guard to go back to the signalbox, and the procedure would then have been for the guard to have written details in the signalbox train register book and for the signalman to have placed a metal lever collar on the Home signal lever to physically prevent him from pulling the lever and to remind him of the standing train. With the widespread installation of track circuits, accidents caused by failure to carry out this rule are much less frequent than they once were, but the worst disaster in the history of railways in Great Britain, at Quintinshill, just north of Gretna Junction, in 1915, would have been prevented if this Rule had been properly carried out.

But to return to the question with which this chapter started — how to protect the stranded train. Many of the safeguards already explained were not devised specifically with the safety of a stranded train in mind, but rather with the protection of trains stopped by signals, or otherwise, in the normal course of train operation.

Furthermore they only apply on lines worked in the traditional manner with lineside signalboxes using the Absolute Block Signalling system. On lines equipped with

Left:
Twin built-in electrically-lit tail-lamps seen here on a Swiss Federal Railways coach at Basle. Note the power-operated plug-type sliding doors. Author

modern signalling and continuous track circuiting, as is now the case on most trunk routes, the stranded train protects itself. By occupying a track circuit, it causes the signal in rear to be held at Danger. But even this may not be enough, as was demonstrated on a line that runs through the very heart of peaceful commuter-land from Marylebone to High Wycombe. During a snowstorm on the morning of 11 December 1981 one diesel multiple-unit ran into the back of another which had been brought to a stand by tree branches bending low over the line due to the weight of snow on them. The driver and three passengers were killed. The circumstances of this collision, near Seer Green, are explained in detail in Chapter 6, but the first train had only been standing for a few minutes when the collision occurred — insufficient time for detonator protection by the guard to be effective.

Could anything more be done to protect a standing train? There are two aspects to this — one is to make a standing train more conspicuous to another train approaching it, the driver of which knows it to be somewhere in the vicinity; the other is to give emergency, last minute warning to an approaching driver that he is running into unknown but imminent danger.

There was a long-held belief that it was perfectly satisfactory for trains to sneak about unnoticed like thieves in the night and that there was no need to illuminate the front and rear, other than to tell signalmen what class a train was, and that it had not left part of itself behind in the section. The tail lamp came to be vital, not to warn a following train, but to tell the signalman in the days before continuous track circuiting that it was complete and that the section it had just passed through was clear and safe for another train to pass. The view was firmly held that there was no need for trains to be conspicuous, as the signalling system would ensure that they were kept apart, and that men working on the line should look out for their own safety by keeping their eyes and ears open. Traces of these

beliefs still linger on, for how else can one explain the railway's love affair with the oil-lit tail lamp, which is only slowly going out of use, or the miserable little lights on the front of locomotives and multiple-units, which are only gradually being reinforced by the use of penetrating headlights? Having said that, the oil tail lamp has many advantages — it is cheap to make, easy to use, has low running costs, and does not go dim if the train's batteries run down. It is very reliable and gives quite a good light too, being clearly visible at half a mile on a clear night on straight track (and no matter how good a tail light is, it cannot be seen round corners). However, a number of factors are combining to push it into the museum — the rise in the cost of lamp oil, the cost of storage and distribution, fears about future difficulties in obtaining supplies of lamp oil when BR is the only large user, and the heavy labour cost of cleaning, filling and trimming oil lamps. But more than anything it is BR's foresight in equipping nearly all locomotives and multiple-units with twin electrically-operated, built-in tail lamps that is forcing the issue (coupled with the huge reduction in the number of freight trains, which were the heaviest user of oil tail lamps) and the realisation since the Rule was altered to require both to be lit, that twin tail lights present a much more visually arresting and easily recognisable image than a single light. The problem that remains concerns locomotive-hauled trains. It is to be hoped that all new coaches designed for locomotive haulage will have twin built-in tail lamps, but the existing coaches will be in use for many years yet, and freight and parcels trains have to be provided for. The contrast between twin electric tail lights and a single oil-lit tail light is too great to accept and the search is on for an acceptable substitute. Paradoxically, the problem is made more difficult because the numbers required are not huge, therefore they do not benefit from the much lower unit production cost which would apply if larger numbers were required. To put two on each train would not double the

Above:
A track circuit operating clip in position in the driver's cab of a DMU, ready for emergency use. Author

Below:
A track circuit operating clip in use, short-circuiting the electric current of the track circuit and activating automatic safeguards. Ian Allan Library

total cost but it would create difficult handling problems. Battery-lit tail lamps are quite cumbersome and heavy and often have to be handled from ground level and it is unrealistic to suggest that there should be two on each train. It would, however, be reasonable to have two on every passenger train, as is widely practised on continental railways, but for other trains it rather appears that a single tail lamp has to be accepted, with as bright a light as can be realistically achieved. It is often suggested that tail lamps should flash on and off in order to be more visually arresting than a steady light, and this may provide the answer where only one lamp is used, and might help to avoid those rear-end collisions which occasionally occur on lines known as 'permissive' where freight trains are allowed to follow one behind the other. Even on the continent there is no universal practice — some railways use flashing tail lamps, some do not. BR has been testing a number of types of electric battery-operated tail lamps which emit a flashing light, one of which is extensively used on the Deutsche Bundesbahn (the German Federal Railway). Another type has been developed by the BR Research Department in conjunction with private industry, and has eight LEDs (light-emitting diodes). BR hopes to replace all oil tail lamps by the late 1980s with electric battery-operated lamps.

The guards of the stranded trains at Invergowrie and Seer Green must have wished they had some means of alerting the drivers of the approaching trains that they were running into danger. Radio may seem at first sight to be an answer, but would it have been of practical value with so

Left:
The emergency services at work after the Micheldever accident of 26 January 1985, when Class 33/1 No 33104 running light engine wrong-line from Worting Junction collided with the stranded 03.30 Bournemouth-Woking electric multiple unit which it had been sent to rescue. Simon N. Rowley

use in a lifetime's career? Would it be readily available for use at literally a second's notice? (in other words guards would have to carry it with them at all times). Would it work without fail? Would guards know how it worked? Small distress-flares of the type used by mountaineers and sailors would meet most of the requirements — they are cheap, could be renewed periodically, would be available at a second's notice and would immediately alert the driver of an approaching train, but would guards feel happy to be carrying them around in their pockets? Probably not, but the same objections could be made against detonators, which guards have always carried around, and a dozen detonators are surely more hazardous than one or two small flares. However, railway traditions die very hard and flares are unlikely to be adopted unless there is a sudden spate of 'Invergowries', or unless supplies of detonators dry up — a distinct possibility. Since the use of detonators for fog signalling was discontinued in 1981, BR's requirements for supplies of detonators have declined to such an extent that it is hardly worth a manufacturer's while to produce them. What is more, they do not find favour with the Railway Inspectorate owing to the risk of injury to the user by flying fragments, nor with the police because they are stolen from railway premises in quite large numbers. So one day flares may replace detonators, and another piece of railway history will be consigned to the museum. It is interesting to recall that Col Pringle, reporting on the Ais Gill crash of 1913, discussed at some length the use of flares as a means of protecting a stranded train, in fact he made a firm recommendation that flares should be carried in all guards' vans, but before the railway companies could properly consider this proposal, events were overtaken by the more urgent worries of World War 1.

The best safeguard of all is modern signalling with AWS and continuous track-circuiting. Track circuiting also allows the use of a simple but effective piece of emergency warning equipment, carried in every driving cab and brakevan, consisting of two spring clips connected by a short piece of wire, and known appropriately as a track circuit operating clip. When one of the clips is placed over one rail and the other clip over the other rail the weak electric current of the track circuit is diverted through the wire, resulting in a short-circuit that is detected by the signalling equipment, which in turn switches to Danger the signal in rear (or holds it at Danger if it is already showing a red aspect). It also alerts the signalman to the fact that an emergency may have arisen. Initially it proved quite difficult to get traincrews to use track circuit operating clips as an instinctive reaction in an emergency, a situation commented on in a number of Department of Transport Railway Inspecting Officers' Reports, and the problem was only solved by prominently displaying a notice in every driving cab, alongside the track circuit operating clip, saying 'Protection of line — use track circuit operating clip first'. At first there were doubts as to the effectiveness of the clip, but extensive tests in different parts of the country, at various times of the year, showed an effectiveness of over 99% — better even than detonators.

Detonators may seem old-fashioned, indeed they are old-fashioned, but they have many advantages — they are cheap, quick and easy to use, foolproof, effective, small and easily carried, instantly available for use and have a long

little time available? There may have been time for the signalmen concerned in both accidents to have contacted the drivers with an emergency call, but there was surely insufficient time for the train crews of the stranded trains to have contacted the drivers of the approaching trains — they would have lost vital seconds in getting to their radio equipment and more in making contact; but it is a facility which *could* be valuable if designers of radio equipment could incorporate such a feature.

There are problems in designing emergency warning equipment if it is only to be used on very rare occasions. The circumstances of Invergowrie are comparatively rare, which means that the vast majority of guards are never faced with them. Is it a practical proposition to provide emergency equipment that 19 out of 20 guards may never

life. Whilst their use on BR is declining they are still invaluable in some situations where there is at present no obvious alternative. One of their many uses is the secondary protection of a stranded train. The main protection, against the approach of a train which ought not to be there, has already been described. The secondary protection is against the assisting locomotive, which has a right to be approaching, but whose driver may not know exactly where the stranded train is standing, and whose forward view may be limited during fog, or at night, or by the curvature of the line in cuttings or through overbridges, etc. To guard against the possibility of a collision between the assisting locomotive and a stranded train, detonators are placed on the line 300yd from the train in both directions. In addition, the guard or driver of the stranded train is required to travel with the driver of the assisting locomotive to guide him safely towards the train. This procedure should be foolproof but occasionally there are collisions, through carelessness, or because the Rules were not being properly observed or even because the assisting locomotive was being driven at too high a speed. On 23 May 1981 the locomotive of a passenger train ran out of fuel between Neath and Swansea and another locomotive was sent to assist. Both locomotives were damaged when the assisting locomotive collided with the failed one. The driver of the stranded train had failed to put down his secondary detonator protection because he thought the guard had done so. The guard of the stranded train should have preceded the assisting locomotive on foot for the last 300yd (ie from the detonators which ought to have been there but were not) but in the absence of detonators had no warning as to where he should alight, and the assisting locomotive was being driven too fast.

A somewhat similar case occurred near Micheldever on the Waterloo-Basingstoke-Southampton main line during the small hours of 26 January 1985. The 03.30 Bournemouth-Woking, consisting of three four-car electric multiple-units, and conveying a number of railway staff as passengers, struck a minor chalk slip in the cutting between the two Popham Tunnels. Some of the train's current-collector shoes were damaged and it lost power,

finally coming to a stand with the front two coaches outside the tunnel mouth. The guard went to the front of the train to confer with the driver, in accordance with the rules, and it was arranged that the guard would go back to protect his train in the rear and advise the signalman of the situation. This he did, and the signalman told him that he would arrange for a light locomotive to be sent to the front of the train, and that the guard should arrange for someone to go forward and meet it 300yd ahead. The relief locomotive, No 33104, set off from Worting Junction, running in the down direction over the Up line, initially at about 50mph but slowing down to about 25/30mph when about a mile from the disabled train. The driver was keeping a sharp lookout for the red light which should have been shown 300yd from the disabled train, when the train itself suddenly loomed up out of the darkness only a few yards away. There was no time for the driver to brake and he smashed into the stationary train at about 30mph, injuring both himself and his assistant.

The accident resulted from several failures to carry out the rules properly. The driver of the disabled train should have put down detonators 300yd in front of his train and stayed there, showing a red light, but he omitted to do either; the signalman should not have allowed the assisting locomotive to proceed towards the disabled train until he had received an assurance that there was someone at the 300yd protection point — he received no such assurance; and the assisting locomotive was being driven too fast. The fundamental principle of railway safety is that there is more than one line of defence, so that if the first line of defence fails there is a second, to act as a safety net. At Micheldever there were no fewer than three lines of defence, and all failed. Protection by the driver was the first, the signalman was the second, and the driver of the assisting locomotive the third, although he could hardly have avoided a collision in the circumstances but he might have been able to reduce its force. Each man was anxious to get the trains moving as quickly as possible and each man allowed those very worthy considerations to override the needs of safety; by no means an unusual occurrence, as these pages show.

3 Permanent Speed Limits

People on holiday, in Spain or Italy perhaps, may occasionally wonder, while lazing in the sun, whether everything is all right back home. Their thoughts may turn idly to the possibility of being burgled, or of having a burst water pipe. But whatever horrors they may contemplate it is unlikely that anyone in their wildest dreams would ever visualise returning home to find their house damaged by what can only be described as a low-flying train.

The 19.50 sleeping car express from Aberdeen to King's Cross on Saturday 23 June 1984, the 'Night Aberdonian', consisted of seven almost new Mk 3 sleeping cars, with a parcels van at each end of the train. The locomotive was Class 47/4 diesel-electric No 47452. It left Aberdeen on time and made its usual scheduled stops as far as Edinburgh Waverley, where the traincrew were relieved and a fresh set of men (driver and guard) took over. At 23.05, still on time, it set off on the next leg of its journey, non-stop to Newcastle.

The route from Edinburgh to Newcastle is very picturesque, particularly in its early stages where it closely follows the coast, but it suffers from an unusually large number of speed restrictions round curves, one of the most

severe being a 50mph restriction through Morpeth station. Although the locomotive had a maximum permitted speed of 95mph the train was timed somewhat more slowly than this in the interest of the greater comfort of the sleeping car passengers, and it was not really necessary to travel at more than about 80mph in order to keep time, although the train could quite safely have been driven at speeds of up to 95mph on suitable stretches of the line if it had been necessary to regain lost time. However on the night of Saturday 23/Sunday 24 June 1984 it was running on time.

The journey was uneventful until the train was approaching Morpeth just before 00.40. All the speed-restricted curves had been safely negotiated, including the severe one through Berwick-upon-Tweed and over the Royal Border Bridge, but the train did not make its customary slowing as it approached Morpeth station and

Below:
Class 40 No 258 takes a northbound coal train through the curve at Morpeth on 17 July 1970. I. S. Carr

the 50mph curve. On the contrary, it continued unchecked at a speed of probably between 85 and 90mph and hurtled through Morpeth station. For a few seconds the train held the rails but then it started to overturn and left them at a tangent. The first vehicles to overturn were probably the leading two sleeping cars. The locomotive came to rest on its side against a bank, having crossed over the Down line, which it destroyed; and the two vehicles following it, a parcels van and the first sleeping car, jack-knifed behind it and came to rest on their sides across both lines, completely blocking the railway. The second sleeping car led the remainder of the train straight towards a group of bungalows, two of which were actually struck and damaged. All the sleeping cars came to rest on their sides except the last one. The residents of one of the bungalows were on holiday in Spain. The residents of the other had a rather more immediate shock.

Incredibly, not a single passenger was killed, and even more incredibly not one of the 29 who were taken to hospital was detained. It was a spectacular but extremely expensive demonstration of the safety of design of British Rail's modern sleeping cars. Only the driver and two sleeping-car attendants were detained in hospital. There were no fatalities.

But why did the driver fail to reduce speed for the Morpeth curve? Lt-Col A. G. Townsend-Rose, the Inspecting Officer who held a Public Inquiry into the accident, concluded that:

'. . . the driver had clearly failed to properly control his train. There are two possible reasons for this; that he suffered a severe bout of coughing shortly before he should have begun to reduce the train's speed (as had been suggested in the evidence given) and that he remained incapable until the train overturned. It seems that the driver had never reported to the Railway Medical Officers the fact that he suffered from an incapacitating coughing condition. In any case he had only to take his feet off the DSD pedal (the Driver's Safety Device — usually referred to

as the "Deadman's Pedal") to stop the train if he had begun to cough uncontrollably and he could also have shut off power and applied the brakes very quickly. Alternatively it is possible that he became drowsy and inattentive because of the drink he had taken. Although he may have failed to reduce the train's speed sufficiently for the 65mph restriction some 13 miles north of Morpeth, he was alert enough to sound his horn . . . seven miles further on. In the last six miles approaching Morpeth at some 80mph or more he may have fallen asleep, or become so drowsy that he completely forgot about the approaching curve. I must say that I am strongly inclined to the possibility that he fell fully or nearly asleep as being the most likely.'

It is not unknown for people to feel drowsy after sitting quietly for some time, whether they have taken drink or not, and irrespective of the hour of day or night. Car drivers sometimes feel drowsy on long journeys, especially on motorways, and occasionally crashes occur as a result. Many people will recognise the feeling of involuntarily 'nodding off', in fact it is such a common experience that one might expect some kind of safeguard to be provided on a locomotive.

Everyone knows about the 'Deadman's handle' or pedal, which has to be kept depressed by the driver. If pressure is released, power is shut off and the brake is automatically applied. It is a powerful safeguard, provided on all locomotives and multiple-units, and generally very effective in case of unconsciousness and death, although these are fortunately rare occurrences. It is not, however, particularly effective in cases of drowsiness or momentary periods of light sleep when the muscles have not had time to relax sufficiently to enable the spring-loaded handle or foot-pedal to overcome the weight of the hand or foot. Whether it would be effective during a severe bout of coughing is not known. It is also susceptible to misuse, highly irregular though that might be.

Automatic Warning Signalling (AWS) is another powerful safeguard against lack of attention caused by drowsiness

Above:
The locomotive and leading vehicle of the Up 'Night Aberdonian', which came to grief on the Morpeth curve shortly after midnight on Sunday 24 June 1984. S. Miller

Top right:
A Mk 3 sleeping car. The strength of the Mk 3 body shell undoubtedly contributed to the remarkably low casualty figures, with no fatalities and not a single passenger seriously injured. British Rail

Above right:
The overturned sleepers of the 'Night Aberdonian' lie in the front garden belonging to one of the houses adjoining the line. S. Miller

Right:
A remarkable aerial photograph showing how the derailed 'Night Aberdonian' headed straight as an arrow towards the two bungalows, and narrowly avoided destroying both of them. London Express News & Feature Services

or 'nodding off'. It too is not foolproof, as we have already seen, but the sound of the warning horn as the driver passes a Caution signal is normally sufficient to bring him back to his senses, and if it does not the automatic brake will stop the train safely. Even at the end of a journey approaching a terminal station the last signal will show at least a Caution aspect, to prevent a drowsy driver from crashing at speed into the buffers. However, there were no special safeguards approaching the Morpeth curve from the north.

To see why this was so, we need to look back over the last 30 years to study the accidents that have had a bearing on this subject, and examine their special features. The first one to be considered occurred at Sutton Coldfield on 23 January 1955 when a Sunday express, the 12.15pm York-Bristol, consisting of 10 coaches hauled by Class 5 4-6-0 No 45274, which was being diverted from its normal

Above:
The scene today, after repairs to both the track and the bungalows. The severity of the curve can clearly be seen in this photograph. Author

route via Tamworth, was derailed when passing over the 30mph speed-restricted curve through the station at between 55 and 60mph. The casualty list was high by today's standards: 14 passengers and 3 railwaymen were killed. A total of 23 were detained in hospital. The salient features of this accident compared with the Morpeth derailment were:

1 Speed was only 25-30mph in excess of the restriction, and restrictions normally had a built-in safety margin to allow for drivers misjudging their speeds on locomotives not equipped with speedometers.
2 There was no 'Deadman's Pedal', as the locomotive involved was a steam locomotive.
3 The locomotive was double-manned.
4 There was no AWS on the line or on the locomotive.
5 The accident occurred at 4.13pm in full daylight on a fine clear day.
6 There were no lineside warning signs about the speed restriction.
7 There was no comfortable stuffy cab to cause the driver to 'nod-off'.

The driver and fireman were both killed and it is impossible to say why the driver overlooked the speed restriction. At that time it was not the practice on lines of the former London Midland & Scottish Railway to erect lineside signs at speed restrictions, there being no apparent need. There had been only one previous serious derailment of this type (in 1931 at Carlisle Canal Junction on the LNER) since before World War 1, and awareness of speed restrictions was considered to be part of a driver's normal route knowledge. A driver was, and still is, required to be completely familiar with a route before he is allowed to drive a train over it. However, as a result of the Sutton Coldfield accident the British Transport Commission (forerunners of British Railways) decided to erect lineside cut-out signs at the beginning of each speed restriction, depicting the speed allowed. They were intended to serve only as markers, and not as safeguards against a driver who had forgotten to reduce speed. Cut-out signs of this type were already provided on lines of the former London & North Eastern Railway. The Great Western Railway had also given some consideration to this problem and had provided illuminated notices of various types at places where speed restrictions required special emphasis, or where there were no distinctive landmarks.

When the railways were nationalised, the Railway Executive, as part of a process of reviewing the former private companies' safety arrangements with a view to standardisation, recommended the provision of indication signs at the commencement of speed restrictions where there were no landmarks or where there was experience of persistent excessive speed. It was felt that whilst illumination of the signs would improve matters, it was not essential. However, no action was taken because the new regime soon found itself faced with financial problems. In any case, the curve at Sutton Coldfield would hardly have qualified for a sign under either condition.

Some time after British Railways had decided to erect cut-out signs at the beginning of speed restrictions they decided to mark the termination point also of permanent speed restrictions on high speed lines (maximum speeds of 90mph or more), so providing an indication of every change of speed, either upwards or downwards.

The extreme rarity of this type of accident at the time (1955) might be thought not to have justified any further action; in fact it is difficult to see what more could effectively and realistically have been done, given the available technology and financial resources, apart from erecting illuminated warning signs at braking distance from speed restrictions. However, this would have been

expensive, and a driver who was sufficiently drowsy to be unaware of an approaching severe curve may well have failed to notice the warning sign. An additional safeguard was needed, of a type that the driver could not overlook, and that was to come later as we shall see.

In the Sutton Coldfield accident neither the fireman nor the guard was effective in braking the train for the curve. We cannot know what, if anything, the fireman did, but the action that the guard took to apply the brake was ineffective. We have noticed before, and we shall notice again, cases where guards were reluctant to intervene; what we do not know, and what there are no means of knowing, is the number of occasions when the guard *has* saved the day. The driver is not likely to report his own failing, and the guard is equally unlikely to report his mate.

Without additional safeguards it was both perfectly obvious and inevitable that sooner or later there would be a repeat of the Sutton Coldfield disaster, although based on experience it was likely to be many years. After all, it had been 24 years since the previous case, but as it happened there wasn't very long to wait. By coincidence, the train concerned, the 10.15pm sleeper from King's Cross to

Above left:
The driving cab of a Class 47 locomotive, the type used in the Morpeth derailment.
1 **AWS visual indicator.**
2 **Brake valve for train and locomotive.**
3 **Air brake for locomotive only.**
4 **Gauges for brake pressure, engine rpm and speed.**
5 **Power controller.**
6 **Forward, idling and reverse controller.**
7 **Warning horn.**
Ian Allan Library

Left:
'Deadman's pedal', on the floor beneath the desk of a Class 86 electric locomotive. Author

Below:
Disaster in a quiet suburb on a Sunday afternoon. The wreckage of the 12.15 York-Bristol express at Sutton Coldfield on 23 June 1955. T. Gladdy

Edinburgh, was also being diverted from its normal route because of engineering works. Approaching Lincoln on the diversionary route there is a very severe curve which is restricted to 15mph, but the train was still travelling at 55mph when it hit the curve. Seven coaches overturned, two passengers and a sleeping car attendant were killed and 49 were injured. The date was Sunday 3 June 1962, the time 12.49. Fortunately in this accident the driver survived to give his evidence. In fact his locomotive, an English Electric Type 4 2,000hp diesel-electric, was not derailed, and came to a stand in the middle of Lincoln station. He was not a regular driver of main line diesels but had taken duty specially that night to conduct the normal driver of the express over the diversionary route, as the normal driver was not acquainted with it. The conductor driver was fully aware of the speed restriction approaching Lincoln but it is thought that he may have misjudged his speed. It is easy to imagine how that could happen; drivers of steam locomotives had always been accustomed to estimating their speed by the feel of the locomotive, and by the noise and vibration. A driver who had spent perhaps 40 years on steam locomotives, and then found himself on a diesel, and who then estimated his speed in the traditional way instead of by glancing at his speedometer, could so easily overspeed in the dark, given the smoothness and quietness of a nearly new diesel locomotive with power shut off and the engine just ticking over.

However, there was clearly an element of doubt in Col Reed's mind, when he reported on the accident after holding a Public Inquiry. He concluded:

'. . . after making all possible allowances, it is difficult to accept that he had firmly intended to reduce speed to the required limit of 15mph at the junction, and that the actual speed of about 55mph was wholly due to misjudgement.'

Col Reed did not speculate what else it might have been due to. It is interesting to note from the evidence in the Report that the signalman at Sincil Bank signalbox, almost opposite the point where the derailment occurred, had not

Above:
The magical 100mph. The cut-out sign being erected for the first stretch on the East Coast main line between Stoke Summit and Lolham, which started with the summer timetable of 1964. Cloth caps were *de rigueur* in the days before high-visibility vests.
British Railways (ER)

Left:
The '125' era arrives.
The Scotsman

Right & far right:
The 60mph permanent speed restriction warning sign on the Up main line at Carlisle Kingmoor, together with its warning magnet. Author

placed his level crossing gates across the road and cleared his Home signal until the train was almost at it, yet the train passed him at about 55mph. It is obvious that the driver could not have stopped at the Home signal if it had remained at Danger. There was a lineside cut-out sign at the commencement of the curve, and one can only speculate whether a warning indicator at braking distance from the curve would have been effective, with or without an AWS magnet to remind the driver. If the overspeeding was entirely due to misjudgement it would not have been effective, but if there was some other cause, eg inattention, it might well have prevented the accident.

The guard of the express was also not the regular guard, but like the driver had come on duty specially to conduct the train over the diversion between Peterborough and Doncaster. He was travelling in the ninth vehicle and began to get worried about the speed of the train as it approached Lincoln. He rose from his seat to apply the brake but before he could do so he felt the lurch caused by the derailment. Col Reed felt that in the particular circumstances he was not to blame for not having applied the brake.

The inability to form any real conclusions about the true cause of the Lincoln derailment naturally made it more difficult to propose any remedial action. The provision of an advanced warning indicator at braking distance from the curve might have been effective but it was also felt that the element of risk would diminish as drivers became more accustomed to diesel locomotives, and that the circumstances of the Lincoln derailment were unlikely to recur. There was no real evidence to justify substantial expenditure on warning indicators all over the railway system, yet, without any further precautions, and with entire reliance upon the driver's knowledge of a route, and on his constant alertness, there remained a loophole in the railway's safety defences which, sooner or later, was bound to lead to tragedy. How long it would take was impossible to say, given the dates of previous derailments on curves — 1931, 1955 and now 1962.

When it did finally happen, on 7 May 1969, the face of British Railways had changed completely. Steam loco-motives had disappeared, colour-light signalling and AWS were widespread, and Dr Beeching had departed, leaving his shadow across the land. The circumstances of the accident were uncannily like those of the 1984 derailment at Morpeth. The train concerned, the Down 'Aberdonian' 19.40 sleeping car express from King's Cross to Aberdeen, was the sister of the one involved in 1984. The driver entered a 40mph speed-restricted curve at slightly over 80mph (85-90mph in the 1984 accident), at 01.31 (00.40 in 1984). And finally the wrecked train came to rest at the identical location — just south of Morpeth station. Truth is indeed stranger than fiction. But similarities cease there because in 1969 six people were killed and 19 seriously injured.

The Down 'Aberdonian' on 7 May 1969 left Newcastle at 01.06, seven minutes late. It consisted of 11 vehicles marshalled as follows:

1 Guard's van
2 Sleeping cars
4 Coaches
1 Guard's van
2 Sleeping cars
1 Brake coach.

All the vehicles were of Mk 1 design and they were all buckeye-coupled. The oldest was built in 1957. The locomotive was Class 55 diesel-electric 'Deltic' No 9011 *The Royal Northumberland Fusiliers*, and was double-manned by a driver and secondman who had taken over at Newcastle at the start of their turn of duty. The journey from Newcastle to the Morpeth curve was perfectly normal. The driver said in his evidence at the Public Inquiry that the night was dark but very clear. He observed all speed restrictions including one at Cramlington, and then, with all signals at Green he opened the controller fully and accelerated to 80mph. He closed the controller at the usual place for the Morpeth curve and thought that he must then have begun to think about an official letter that he had been handed when signing-on, asking for an explanation of four

minutes lost on a previous journey. He thought that he had allowed his attention to wander, and he was brought round, and made a full brake application, just as he hit the curve. The locomotive rode the curve very well (as at Lincoln in 1962) and he thought that the train had also done so safely until he looked back when the locomotive stopped, and saw the wreckage behind him. How his heart must have sunk! One cannot help but sympathise with him in his awful predicament. A few moments inattention, and a wrecked train. A heavy price for a simple human failing and an illustration yet again of the heavy responsibilities carried at that time by drivers day in and day out.

And what of the secondman? By the time he realised that the train was going too fast for the curve, and that the brakes were not being applied, they were closely approaching it. Despite an understandable unwillingness to appear to be interfering, that may be thought natural in a secondman in such conditions, he started to move across the cab of the locomotive to warn the driver, when he was thrown to the floor by the lurch of the locomotive entering the curve. He had acted too late, but the Inspecting Officer, Col J. R. H. Robertson, found that he was not to blame for that. Anyone who might be tempted to think otherwise should put himself in the secondman's shoes and ask himself whether he would have acted differently *without the benefit of hindsight*. At 84mph there were only a few seconds for him to reach a positive decision. The practice of carrying a secondman on night trains was later abandoned. It proved to be of no practical value. Accidents happened with two men in the cab and it was not unknown for both to 'nod-off', the one relying on the other to keep alert. Two men are carried in the cabs of trains travelling at over 100mph at any time, but they are both drivers and the circumstances are somewhat different, as will be discussed in a later chapter.

Morpeth 1969 proved to be a landmark in the long history of railway safety. As had happened so often before, a serious accident provided the necessary impetus for remedial action. No sensible man could any longer doubt that safety at speed-restricted curves ought to be improved if suitable means could be found of doing so. It was no longer enough just to be sure that drivers were well aware of such curves. Something was needed to guard against a moment's inattention; and by good fortune the means had become readily available. The installation of AWS was by this time proceeding rapidly and nearly all locomotives had been equipped with receiver apparatus. What could be easier than to install an AWS permanent magnet in the track just at the place where a driver would normally start to brake? Then, if the driver was inattentive the sound of the warning horn would alert him. If the driver were temporarily insensible, as may have happened in the 1984 Morpeth derailment, the train would be stopped safely by the automatic application of the brake. Either way, safety would be provided for. So why did the second Morpeth accident occur?

It is one thing to decide to install a permanent magnet on the approach to curves. Nothing easier. But Britain's railway lines are full of curves, and the approaches to major stations are often a mass of speed restrictions. To put a magnet at every one, at braking distance, would need many thousands of magnets. Acknowledgement of the warning by drivers might become routine. It might even, as some feared, become subconscious. The value of the warning might become degraded and as it is the same warning as the one received at a Caution signal, that would be an unacceptable risk. In closely-signalled areas with many speed restrictions drivers would be passing over magnets, sometimes for signals, sometimes for speed restrictions, every few hundred yards, and that could cause confusion. So it was necessary to decide which speed restrictions should be treated and which should not. And thus, the seeds of the second Morpeth accident were sown.

With the Morpeth curve very much in mind, it was felt that there were two factors in the reckoning — the speed of an approaching train and the severity of the speed

restriction. Col Robertson felt that permanent magnets should be installed on all lines where trains were allowed to travel at 75mph or more, wherever a speed restriction demanded a reduction in speed of one-third or more, eg from 90 to 60mph, or 75 to 50mph. In addition an illuminated advanced warning board should be provided 200yd beyond the magnet, braking distance being measured from the board to the start of the restriction.

There were many details of principle to be settled but by November 1972 a total of 47 installations had been completed. Year by year the figure increased until by the end of 1977 there were 318 installations in all, and the programme was complete. The precautions taken, whilst appropriate to the Down line situation at Morpeth, would not have prevented the derailments at either Sutton Coldfield or Lincoln, because in both those cases the approach speeds were limited to 60mph, yet they showed just how destructive derailments can be at that speed. It might be thought therefore that the speed conditions to be satisfied before warning equipment was installed approaching a curve were not sufficiently all-embracing, as many dangerous locations would continue to be unprotected. This was emphasised by another serious high-speed derailment on a curve near Eltham (Well Hall) station on the Southern Region on Sunday 11 June 1972, when a return excursion train from Margate entered a 20mph curve at about 65mph. The train was wrecked, five passengers and the driver were killed, and many people were seriously injured. Col Robertson, who also took this Public Inquiry, concluded that the driver had grossly impaired his ability to drive safely by drinking a considerable quantity of alcohol both before and after booking on duty ... The secondman did not know the route and could not have realised that the driver was not braking for the curve when he should have been.

The curve at Eltham would not have qualified for an Advanced Warning Indicator and permanent magnet, because the approach speed was less than 75mph, and although other safeguards were subsequently applied there, that disaster showed tragically yet again that curves on lines below 75mph could also constitute a hazard. However, at that time BR had only just started to equip high-speed lines. Nevertheless, three out of the last four accidents (Sutton Coldfield 1955, Lincoln 1962 and Eltham 1972) had occurred on relatively low-speed lines (60mph), yet in all three cases the trains were severely damaged and passengers had been killed. It might therefore have been prudent to have started planning for an extension, a second stage, for the installation of Warning Indicators and magnets, to follow completion of the first stage in 1977, but it was not done. Perhaps attention was distracted by the prominence of the drink factor in the Eltham crash, and the need to take immediate and firm measures to deal with it, but in the event it was some years before a second stage began to be considered; and before it could become effective further accidents had happened.

It may seem strange that the Down line at Morpeth was equipped, but not the Up. After all it is the same curve, with the same 50mph restriction, approached at high speed in both directions. But whereas in the Down direction in 1969 the speed limit suddenly dropped by half from 80mph to 40mph (now 50mph), in the Up direction the speed limits fall in stages, from 100mph to 80mph (for ¼ mile), and then to 70mph for ¾ mile, before the 50mph curve is reached. By the Rules of the time none of these changes in speed justified an Advanced Warning Indicator because none of them was more severe than a one-third reduction, therefore no Indicator was provided, other than the standard cut-out. There are many examples of such staged reductions on BR, known as cascades, but when the 'Morpeth Rules' were being drawn up after the 1969 derailment it was felt to be more important to deal with the straightforward cases. The original 'Morpeth Rules' did not deal with all speed restrictions, only the most vulnerable ones, and the Rules have now been amended to take account of severe restrictions of speed where speed is reduced in a series of stages. In general, each stage must be

Left & right:
The sad result of attempting to go round a 20mph curve at 65mph at Eltham (SR) on 11 June 1972. Gary Merrin

considered as if it were from the initial approach speed, and where this is 75mph or more and the total reduction required is one-third or more an Advanced Warning Indicator and permanent magnet must be provided. At Morpeth in the Up direction the total reduction is from 100mph to 50mph and warning equipment has now been installed there.

The new arrangements might well have prevented a serious derailment at Paddington on 23 November 1983, when yet another sleeping car express came to grief. The train was the 21.35 from Penzance, and consisted of 14 coaches and vans, including four sleeping cars, hauled by a Class 50 diesel-electric locomotive No 50041 *Bulwark*. At 06.11 it was approaching Paddington when, instead of slowing down for the crossovers outside the terminus, it continued at speed. It was still travelling at more than 65mph when it entered a 25mph crossover; the locomotive dashed into the sharp curves, with wheel flanges and rails screeching loudly in protest. For a few seconds it clung tenaciously to the rails, rocking violently, but momentum was too strong and it finally lost its grip and became derailed, running on the sleepers for some distance before overturning on to its side. Behind it the train rushed onwards into almost complete derailment — only the last coach stayed on the rails. Incredibly there were no serious injuries and only three passengers were taken to hospital suffering from minor injuries and shock, but the scene outside Paddington station was one of devastation. Many days were to pass before everything was back to normal.

The driver was unhurt and he climbed out of his

locomotive cab unaided. His feelings at that moment can be imagined; the terror he had gone through hurtling forward in his derailed locomotive wondering whether he would survive; his intense relief when he found that he was uninjured, followed by a dreadful apprehension that behind him in the train may lie dead and injured passengers and fellow railwaymen, and finally, perhaps, a frantic search in his mind for the cause of such a disaster.

In his evidence at the Public Inquiry, held by the Chief Inspecting Officer of Railways, Maj C. F. Rose, the driver said that he started to apply the air brake when he was still about 2½ miles from the terminus. As the train did not appear to be slowing he made a full service brake application and finally an emergency application. The gauges in his cab showed maximum brake force but there was still no discernible reduction in speed before the point of derailment.

The most detailed investigations, lasting for many weeks, were carried out into the train's braking system, but nothing could be found to account for the failure. The brakes had worked perfectly at all the station stops between Penzance and Reading, and worked again seconds before the train became derailed. Maj Rose concluded that it was most probable that the driver lost concentration, either through drowsiness or by allowing his mind to wander, and failed to realise how closely and how quickly he was approaching the terminus. If that is what really happened, the 'deadman's pedal' was ineffective, for the same reason as we have seen before in a short period of drowsiness.

Left:
The scene of the Paddington accident on 23 November 1983. The strength and safety of modern coaches and sleepers are clearly shown in this photograph. Although the passengers had a rude awakening, none of them was badly hurt.
Mick Roberts

Top:
The Old Oak Common breakdown crane re-rails one end of Mk 3 sleeping car No 10563 under the glare of floodlights on 23 November. Mick Roberts

Above:
The much-battered *Bulwark* back on the rails on Saturday 26 November. Mick Roberts

The particular significance of the Paddington accident was its disclosure of a situation which was dramatically highlighted by the subsequent accident at Morpeth. HSTs may travel at their maximum speed of 125mph until they are 4½ miles from Paddington. For the next three miles the speed limit is 85mph, then 60mph for a mile, until the station throat is approached, where a 25mph restriction applies through to the platforms. According to the 'Morpeth Rules' then in force, the arrangement of this cascade of speed limits just avoided the need to provide an Advanced Warning Indicator and a permanent magnet — the reduction from 125mph to 85mph is just less than a third (32%), and so is the reduction from 85mph to 60mph (30%). If these speeds were chosen deliberately to avoid the need to provide warning equipment, it was an unfortunate and expensive decision. Approaching Paddington under clear signals, as did the driver of the 21.35 from Penzance, the first AWS warning was at a signal almost at the fatal crossover — effective enough to prevent the train from crashing into the buffers at full speed but not intended to ensure a safe speed through the crossover. The revised 'Morpeth Rules' will do that now.

We have already seen that it is not practicable to extend the 'Morpeth Rules' to cover every restriction of speed. When the original Rules were drawn up after the 1969 accident they were thought to be sufficient at the time, and a great step forward in improving safety, which they were. The new Rules, which also cater for approach speeds between 75 and 60mph, extend the safeguards, but there will always be vulnerable areas just beyond the margin. The question now is whether enough was done after 1969 to prevent further high-speed derailments. Should the circumstances of the Paddington and the second Morpeth derailments have been foreseen and guarded against? Of the four accidents on which a judgement might have been based — Sutton Coldfield 1955, Lincoln 1962, Morpeth 1969 and Eltham 1972 — three occurred on lines with a maximum speed of 60mph, which might be taken as an indication that those were the lines most at risk. There was certainly nothing to indicate an unusual danger at sharp curves approached by a cascade of speed restrictions, and nothing to suggest that the approaches to large stations and terminals, usually approached by cascades, ought to be dealt with specially, Nevertheless, an impartial observer might have detected the illogicality of safeguarding the Morpeth curve in the Down direction and not in the Up, just because there happened to be a cascade in the Up direction. Whilst the original Morpeth Rules did not provide for cascades, might it not have been common sense to have made an exception at Morpeth? Where was the logic in safeguarding a drowsy or inattentive (or incapacitated) driver in the Down direction but not in the Up? The existence of a cascade in one direction was irrelevant in such circumstances.

Whether the Paddington accident could have been forecast is a different matter. There had been no case, certainly this century, of a train failing to slow down when approaching a major terminus, and such an eventuality was thought to be so unlikely that there was no justification for expenditure to guard against it. And if the brakes *had* failed, as the driver consistently maintained, warning equipment would have provided no safeguard. Most efforts to help the driver have so far been directed towards guarding against the effects of drowsiness or inattention, by providing safeguards such as AWS at signals or speed restrictions, or by double-manning. AWS, though invaluable, has been shown to be less than 100% perfect. Double-manning has been shown to be ineffective (Morpeth 1969, Eltham 1972). Should efforts now be concentrated on methods of maintaining the driver in a state of alertness? Equipment to achieve this, known as a Vigilance Device, is provided in the cabs of HSTs[1]. A warning bleep sounds every minute, and if the driver does not respond by releasing and then depressing the 'deadman's pedal' the brakes are automatically applied. Although even this is not entirely foolproof (as demonstrated at Hayes & Harlington), and does not ensure that a driver observes and reacts correctly to every signal, it is a step in the right direction and worthy of development, which indeed BR are doing.

In another respect drivers' responsibilities are being increased. The relentless marketing pressures to reduce end-to-end journey times, and the increased speeds at which trains can travel, may have the effect of increasing the number of occasions on which speed has to be reduced for intermediate speed restrictions. Between Berwick-upon-Tweed and Morpeth, a distance of 50 miles, there are no fewer than 25 changes in the maximum speed allowed, following a similar number between Edinburgh and Berwick, and a driver travelling in places at a speed of two miles a minute is having to adjust his speed (and, more important, having to remember to do so) once a minute on average.

Further north, on the East Coast main line to Edinburgh and Aberdeen, those same pressures to reduce journey times have led the Scottish Region to draw up a separate maximum-speed profile for HSTs, so that full advantage can be taken of their superior riding qualities and lower axle-weights. But in consequence drivers on that route now have to contend with a separate set of speed restrictions for HSTs, superimposed on the existing speed profile. No additional assistance is given to the driver. It has also to be remembered that an express train is normally travelling at, or near, the maximum safe speed, and the only assistance the driver is given, apart from locations with Advanced Warning Indicators, is the lineside cut-out, suitable only for route-learning, and useless otherwise. He has to rely on his route knowledge, as he has always had to do, but with many of his location markers, such as wayside stations and signalboxes, gone. Even the replacement of semaphore signals by colour-light signals, excellent though they are, is not exclusively an improvement; semaphore signals are often distinctive and individually styled, helping a driver to know exactly where he is on a dark night. Colour lights are anonymous. Technology now exists to give the driver a continuous in-cab indication of the speed limit for the section of track he is on, together with advance warning of any reduction required. It might be difficult to justify the cost, especially as the Morpeth-type loophole has been plugged, but speeds are still rising and location-finding is becoming no easier. It might also be a means of withdrawing the second driver from the cab of trains travelling at over 100mph.

How will posterity judge the events described in this chapter? Will it say that BR took responsible action at the appropriate time, or will it say that it took action too late and on too small a scale, giving the impression that it did not really believe in what it was doing? One cannot help feeling that it may be the latter.

---

[1] Class 50 locomotives were fitted with an electronic vigilance device when first introduced into service, but it proved troublesome and unreliable and was removed.

④ Temporary Speed Restrictions

In the previous chapter we were concerned with speed restrictions of a permanent nature, mainly, but not always, round curves, and it is now time to turn our attention to those of a temporary nature, usually imposed for a few weeks only, on track awaiting renewal or repair, or after such work whilst it settles. Such locations are signposted at the lineside at the beginning and end of the restriction, and there is an advance indicator, called a warning board, at braking distance, showing the speed restriction in miles per hour, with a permanent magnet in the track for additional safety, working in conjunction with the locomotive's AWS equipment. All the signs are illuminated at night and drivers are provided each week with booklets (known as 'Weekly Engineering Notices') giving details of restrictions on all routes over which they work. If a restriction has to be applied at short notice a handsignalman is stationed at the warning board and he gives a Caution indication to drivers, supplemented by a warning detonator. In addition a special notice is posted at drivers' depots in the 'Late Notice' case. It all sounds very safe, and it is, but it was not always so.

Is there some malign fate that makes sleeping car expresses appear so often in these pages? If so, it was at work on the night of 5/6 June 1975. The 23.30 sleeper from Euston to Glasgow left on time, with Class 86 electric locomotive No 86242 hauling 12 sleeping cars, a buffet car and two vans. Just beyond King's Langley the locomotive broke down and another one, No 86006, was put on the front, the whole train starting off again 75min late. Despite the trailing weight of the train and the failed locomotive — 667 tons — No 86006 reached full speed and was running at about 80mph as it approached Nuneaton at 01.54. Just south of the station there was a 20mph temporary speed restriction (called a 'slack' in railway parlance) whilst the track layout was being altered. The express hit the slack at unchecked speed and rushed headlong into disaster. No 86006 left the rails almost at once and smashed its way into the station, for several hundred yards. No 86242 actually mounted the platform and came to rest touching the station awning. The coaches at the front of the train were scattered in all directions, some on their sides, whilst those at the rear remained upright and fairly well in line. The last vehicle, a van, came to rest exactly at the spot where No 86006 had first become derailed. Four passengers and two sleeping car attendants died. Altogether 38 people were taken to hospital and 10 were detained with serious injuries.

At the time of the accident it was not the practice to provide a permanent magnet at the warning board but both the driver and his secondman had the printed notice and knew of the slack at Nuneaton, indeed the driver had been over it, at the slow speed required, the night before on a similar train. Regrettably, the lights at the warning board were out on the night of the accident and although both the driver and the secondman said that they were looking for them they did not see them. At the Public Inquiry both men said they then assumed that the restriction had been removed, although they said no word to each other. They were not entitled to make such an assumption, because if the restriction really had been removed the warning board would have remained in position, illuminated, and the figures showing the speed allowed in miles per hour would have been altered to show the normal speed. Such alterations occur frequently, and are provided for in the Rules.

The Inquiry revealed a disturbing state of affairs and there was evidence that the lights at warning and indicator boards often went out, or that the equipment was stolen or vandalised. Drivers were supposed to report such failures, stopping specially in some circumstances, but were not always doing so. On the night in question quite a number of trains passed the warning board when it was defective. Between 22.30 and 00.58 the drivers of six out of 15 trains passing were prepared to say that the speed indication light

Right:
Temporary speed restriction warning signs, showing:
1 **The warning board, with twin flashing white lights. The battery is in the box at the base of the sign. In the bottom right-hand corner of the picture can be seen a hot axlebox detector.**
2 **The '20' sign, which marks the beginning of the restriction. This is at Long Preston (North Yorks).**
3 **The 'T' sign, which marks the end (the termination) of the restriction.** Author

at the warning board was out. All admitted that they had not reported the fact at the first convenient opportunity as they were required to do by the Rules. The day might then still have been saved. The driver of the next train that passed, at about 01.10, said that the speed indication light was out but that the two horizontal warning lights were lit, although they were dimmer than he had seen them on previous occasions. On the next train at about 01.40 neither driver nor secondman saw any lights on the warning board. They should have stopped and told the signalman so that he could warn all other drivers, but they did not do so. Even at this late stage the accident could have been prevented. The driver of the last train before the accident claimed at first to have seen all the lights but later altered his evidence to say that he had not been in a position to see the warning board at all as his train passed by. It seems therefore that sometime between 01.10 and 01.40 the remaining lights at the warning board went out, and from then on the board was not illuminated in any way.

What is one to make of all these drivers, responsible, experienced men, failing to carry out the Rules properly? The Rules provided a safe method of working. There are three possible conclusions — the first one being that drivers' knowledge of the Rules may be unsatisfactory. They are not re-examined at intervals on their knowledge of the Rules, and are relied upon to keep themselves up to date. The second conclusion is that drivers knew full well what they ought to do but had become tired over many years of stopping to report failures which were still occurring. Drivers as a body dislike making out reports; they dislike even more making out reports and seeing no effective remedial action. This is a natural human reaction, not confined to drivers. But to understand is not to condone. It is only remarkable that this sorry state of affairs did not lead to more accidents, but in fact it had been many years since faulty lights at warning boards had caused one. Accidents at speed restrictions in previous years had been caused mainly by the drivers missing the warning board in daylight. The third possible conclusion is touched upon in the Inquiry Report. The driver of the train involved in the accident agreed that his mind had been very much occupied with regaining as much as possible of the lost time. He had been using his driving skill to the maximum to make up lost time and he agreed that this preoccupation might have prevented his giving full consideration to the possible implications of the 'missing' warning board. Perhaps this concern about punctuality, very proper in normal circumstances, also affects the actions of other drivers and makes them reluctant to stop out of course to report what might appear to be minor failures.

Although it had been many years since the warning arrangements for temporary speed restrictions had last featured as a contributory factor in an accident it was necessary to consider whether additional safeguards should be provided. An examination of Continental practice revealed that several railway systems used the automatic warning part of the signalling system, in conjunction with the AWS equipment on the locomotive, at warning boards for temporary speed restrictions, and it was decided to adopt the practice on BR by placing a permanent magnet between the rails just before the warning board so that the driver would always receive a warning on his AWS equipment, which would alert him if he had missed the warning board and would automatically apply the brakes if he failed to react. It seems such an obvious solution that one may wonder why it had not been adopted sooner. One reason was that there was no apparent need, even though the possibility of an accident was always there and could so easily have been guarded against. Another reason was the reluctance to allow what was a part of the signalling apparatus to be used for non-signalling purposes, based on fears about possible unsafe side-effects. A third reason, and possibly the most important, concerned the problem of the complications that could arise if the proposed location for a magnet for a temporary speed restriction should fall near that of an AWS magnet for a signal or a permanent speed restriction, or near a signal itself, or in a junction layout. There were many such practical problems to be

2

3

overcome in the application of the new arrangements, and the instructions to staff on the precise positioning of the warning board and the magnet run to many pages to cover all the different circumstances.

The decision to use permanent magnets at warning boards was very popular with drivers and removed those nagging doubts which they had had from time to time that they may have missed a warning board or misunderstood an entry in the Weekly Engineering Notice, or that the warning board may have been stolen by vandals. Only in one respect are the new arrangements considered by many drivers to be less than satisfactory. Previously the warning board was located at a fixed distance from the slack (eg 1¼ miles where trains run at 100mph or more) and drivers knew exactly how much room they had in which to reduce their speed to the required level. They could then make whatever adjustments were necessary for gradients, dry or wet rail, type of brake, approach speed, etc. However, to help in overcoming the problems which arose in drawing up the new principles to be adopted in deciding precisely where the magnet and warning board should be located, it was thought to be better to change from a fixed distance to a calculated one, based on the braking distance needed to reduce speed to the required level. But it overlooked the fact that each individual train's braking capacity and requirements are different, depending on a multitude of factors, and it puts drivers in a state of uncertainty. They will always have enough braking distance, but frequently too much, without knowing how much. Drivers then have to 'feel' for the lineside indicator at the start of the slack and may sometimes be worried that they have missed it, especially in the dark. It also leads to unnecessary loss of time in running and is an unpopular change with drivers. Both they and their Union, the Associated Society of Locomotive Engineers and Firemen (ASLEF), tried to persuade BR to change back to a fixed distance but they were unsuccessful. BR's view was that the complications which sometimes arise in finding a suitable location for the warning board and magnet make a system based on a fixed distance unsuitable for the very reason that the fixed distance would have to be increased to an extent unknown to the driver in those cases where the warning board has to be put further away from the speed restriction in order to find a suitable location for it. The same anomaly arises, of course, with the system adopted by BR, which is based on braking distance.

The lineside equipment used for indicating the beginning and end of speed restrictions, and the warning boards, together with their illumination, came under some criticism at the Nuneaton Inquiry. Change often comes slowly on Britain's railways. The design of the equipment had altered very little since before World War 1, but trials had been carried out with bottled gas rather than paraffin oil for the lights at the warning board, and this method was coming into widespread use. It gave a brighter light. Bottled gas was used in the Nuneaton lineside boards, and the lights went out because the bottle was exhausted. The correct procedures had not been followed by the staff responsible, which illustrates the hidden perils of change. Ironically, the change from oil to bottled gas had been made to help the driver, but if the lamps at Nuneaton had been oil-lit it is unlikely that they would all have run dry at the same time.

The equipment and its illumination may seem archaic and primitive for such a vital function, but it worked, at least until the Nuneaton accident. It worked because drivers knew they had to be specially alert to pick out the flickering oil lamps. The use of gas-lit bull's-eye lamps at the warning board was really quite a step forward in improving their conspicuousness. But what more could have been done? Let us itemise the requirements:

1 The equipment must be capable of being manhandled to site along the railway line. The three individual items may be up to two miles or more apart.
2 It must be sufficiently robust to withstand all weathers, plus the turbulence caused by passing trains.

Right:
The awful results of human error at Nuneaton on 6 June 1975. The scattered coaches and sleepers of the 23.30 Euston-Glasgow train lie in the wake of the train locomotive, which has mounted the platform. R. J. Lowe

3 It must be capable of being erected on site and stand firmly.

4 It must be as visually arresting as possible, both by day and by night.

5 Thousands are required, so the purchase or manufacturing cost must be kept down.

6 The method of illumination must be as reliable as possible.

7 The equipment, and means of illumination, should require as little attention as possible whilst in use.

BR's Civil Engineering Department set to work to improve the equipment, adopting space-age technology with the use of electric battery-operated light-emitting diodes (LEDs) as the basis of illumination. The new equipment is reliable, being mostly solid-state, the batteries have a very long life, an indicator shows when they are running down, and energy is conserved in two ways — the lights flash on and off rhythmically, and a light-sensitive cell switches them off in good daylight. The new designs are not the perfect answer, but within the constraints listed above they are an improvement. However, they still depend on the human element — they need to be erected firmly in the correctly calculated location; focussed accurately and monitored properly.

Two other improvements followed to help to remove doubts from drivers' minds. The first concerned the removal of a speed restriction earlier than planned and

published, or the non-imposition of a speed restriction which had already been published (owing, for example, to the cancellation of the planned work). In such cases a warning board would still be erected, but instead of the 'speed' panel showing a number (signifying miles per hour) it would carry a special sign to indicate without question that there was no speed restriction in force.

The second improvement concerned a situation which arose from time to time at junctions where a speed restriction applied on only one leg of the junction, but where the warning board had to be erected before the junction in order to give sufficient braking distance. In such cases drivers proceeding on to the unrestricted route also passed the warning board even though it did not apply to their train. Therefore in order to remove any doubt in the driver's mind the warning board now carries an arrow pointing left or right to whichever leg of the junction the speed restriction applies, so that drivers proceeding towards the other leg can continue at the appropriate speed without worry but, more importantly, drivers proceeding on to the speed-restricted leg will be in no doubt that the restriction applies to them.

One last problem remains on those lines where speeds are high — the indicator at the start of the speed restriction is not always sufficiently conspicuous to enable the driver to pick it out with certainty from confusing backgrounds up to a quarter of a mile away, as he needs to do to be able to

reduce his speed safely on the one hand and avoid the loss of time by premature braking on the other. This factor becomes particularly noticeable when the warning board has had to be moved further out to find a suitable location for it. Motorway-style count-down markers, reflectorised but not illuminated, would be of great assistance to the driver but would place increased demands on the Civil Engineer's staff, although only one marker would be needed at, say, a quarter of a mile from the speed restriction, and the additional workload on the platelayers (or trackmen, as they are now called) might be well worth it in the context of the improved train running which would result. The indicator at the start of the restriction itself cannot really be made much larger because it would then be liable to be blown over by high winds or by the draught of a passing train. Furthermore, its size has to be limited so that it can be located safely between adjoining tracks on multi-track sections.

The best solution of all on high-speed lines would be the ability to superimpose the temporary speed restriction warning arrangements on to the in-cab system designed for permanent speed restrictions mentioned in the previous chapter (although lineside marker posts would still be required at the beginning of the restriction to give the driver an aiming point). Primitive warning boards, no matter how improved, hardly fit in with ultra-modern, multi-million pound signalling. It is incongruous to say the least to have a HST costing millions running smoothly on track costing millions, guided safely by signalling costing millions, yet having to rely for the safe reduction of speed at a temporary restriction on rudimentary equipment costing a few pounds.

Below:
Nuneaton — the early hours of 6 June 1975 and BR recovery crews attempt to sort out the tangle of broken rails and de-railed sleepers. Ian Allan Library

 Procedures at Stations

Easter Monday 1979. The 19.40 electric passenger train from Glasgow to Wemyss Bay was approaching Gilmour Street station, Paisley, under clear signals. To the driver at the controls it was just another routine day, another familiar journey. Neither he nor his passengers had the remotest idea that tragedy and death lay immediately ahead.

At the same moment the 18.58 special passenger train from Ayr to Glasgow was standing in the station waiting for departure time, the passengers tired but happy, returning to Glasgow after a day out at the seaside. Some were dozing, some were reading, while others were just relaxing after the day's exertions. None had any inkling of impending disaster. The guard was standing at the doorway of his van waiting for passengers to finish getting in and out. The driver was sitting quietly at the controls waiting for the 'rightaway' signal. On the platform the leading railman was getting ready to signal to the guard that station duties were complete. The last few moments of absolute normality were slipping by.

Finally the leading railman raised his arm to signal to the guard that all the carriage doors were closed. The guard rang the bell to the driver, and the train moved off. The final, fatal events had been acted out. A few seconds later the two trains met violently head-on and seven people were killed.

What happened was quite simple. According to the Department of Transport Accident Report the driver of the train from Ayr to Glasgow had unwittingly driven his train past a Danger signal at the end of the platform. After that it was purely a matter of fate that the paths of both trains should cross at the same precise instant. If either train had been a few seconds earlier or later it would have been a near miss instead of a collision. That is the way with accidents. Trains had been driven past platform starting signals at Danger on many occasions (there were 36 known cases in 1977/78 alone), and although such errors did not often result in a collision it was clearly only a matter of

Below:
A 1986 view showing the scene of the accident which took place on Easter Monday 1979. Signal P31, seen above, was wrongly passed at Danger by the Ayr-Glasgow DMU, which then collided head-on with a Glasgow-Wemyss Bay EMU just as it was taking the route shown in this photograph. At the time of the accident there were four tracks east of Paisley but they have since been reduced to two. Author

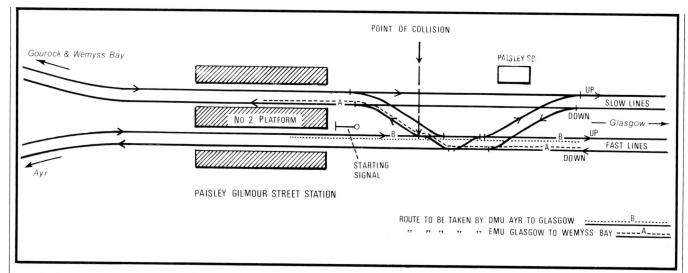

POINT OF COLLISION

Gourock & Wemyss Bay

PAISLEY SB

A

NO 2 PLATFORM

UP
SLOW LINES
DOWN
— Glasgow →
UP
FAST LINES
DOWN

B

B

A

STARTING
SIGNAL

Ayr

PAISLEY GILMOUR STREET STATION

ROUTE TO BE TAKEN BY DMU AYR TO GLASGOW ....B..........
" " " " " EMU GLASGOW TO WEMYSS BAY -----A-----

time before there would be another crash in which people would be killed.

However, before going further it would be useful to examine the procedures for starting trains from stations, as laid down in the British Railways Rule Book. There are three people involved in the operation — the person in charge of the platform, the guard and the driver — and their duties at the time of the Paisley accident were as follows:

Person in charge of the platform
He must see that passengers have joined and alighted, that all parcels traffic has been dealt with, that all doors are closed, that everything is in order and that it is time for the train to leave. He must then indicate this to the guard by giving him the 'All right' signal (either arm held above the head, or at night a white light held above the head).

The Guard
He must satisfy himself that everything is in order so far as he is concerned, and then give a signal to the driver that the train is ready to start. By day he waves a green flag, and by night he shows a steady green light. On multiple-unit trains, instead of using a flag or lamp, the guard presses a button which sounds a bell or buzzer in the driving cab. (To simplify matters the term 'bell' will be used throughout.)

The Driver
His job is specifically to observe and obey signals. He normally takes no part in station activities and merely waits for the indication from the guard that the train is ready to go.

All this sounds very simple and straightforward, and it often is, but what happens on curved platforms where the driver cannot see the guard, or where the station is unstaffed, as many are these days? Or at busy stations with crowded platforms?

Curved Platforms
If the driver cannot see the guard's signal, the person-in-charge of the platform must pass on to the driver the guard's signal, using a green light at night, but by day he has to give the 'All right' signal (one arm above the head) because he doesn't have a green flag.

Unstaffed Stations
The guard has to carry out all platform duties, although most trains stopping at unstaffed stations are fairly short ones. Platform staff are usually on duty where long trains are dealt with.

At busy Stations
To overcome the difficulty of the driver not being able positively and correctly to identify the 'ready to start' signal from the guard or station staff when the platform is crowded or when his line of sight is obstructed by structures or barrow loads of parcels, an electrical indicator, known as a 'Ready to start' indicator, is installed near the locomotive, usually next to the platform starting signal and acting in conjunction with it. When the train is ready to start and the guard has given his signal, the person in charge of the platform operates the 'Ready to start' button which causes the indicator to show an illuminated 'R' to the driver when the signal is clear. If the signal is at Danger no 'R' can be shown and this neatly avoids the Paisley problem. With multiple-units the bell is used instead of the indicator.

The cause of accidents of the Paisley type is known in railway circles as 'Ding-ding, and away' and has a long, long history. As long ago as 1957 Brig Langley of the Railway Inspectorate, Department of Transport, had said in his Report following a Public Inquiry into the collision at Staines Central on 9 August of that year that there had been a number of accidents caused by drivers unwittingly setting off against platform starting signals at Danger after receiving the guard's 'rightaway' signal and that from time to time consideration had been given to altering the Rules so as to require the guard not to give the driver the signal to start if the platform starting signal was at Danger, but he thought that this would imply a measure of dual responsibility for the observance of signals which might cut across the long-established Rule that it is the fundamental responsibility of the driver. He did not recommend any change to the Rules but he did point out the great psychological effect of the guard's 'rightaway' signal, shown by the way drivers had on occasion allowed themselves to be misled by it. However, he thought it desirable that guards and station staff should *where practicable* wait until the platform starting signal had been cleared before giving 'rightaway', and, where they couldn't see the signal, conditions should be reviewed to see whether they could be improved, especially at busy junctions. The railway's response to this was lukewarm but after pressure from Brig Langley they agreed to see what could be done, if only minor expenditure was involved in such improvements.

The question continued to crop up. In 1967 following a similar collision between a Manchester-Bury electric train and a freight train there was some support within railway circles for a change to the Rules, yet even though there were

Above:
Barrier Bell, Right Away, and Train Ready to Start plungers on platforms 4/5 at King's Cross. Author

Above right:
'Off' indicator at King's Cross, which shows that the platform Starting signal has been cleared. Author

Right:
'Off' indicator on the footbridge at Carlisle. This photo graphically demonstrates the problems on crowded, curved platforms. Author

two other accidents that year of the 'Ding-ding, and away' type — at Birmingham Snow Hill and at Bournemouth — no change was made. Five years later Maj Rose of the Department of Transport held a Public Inquiry into a derailment at Clapham Junction on 7 September 1972 and concluded that the driver had unwittingly gone past the platform starting signal at Danger on receipt of the 'rightaway', which incidentally was given by platform staff rather than by bell from the guard. He reiterated Brig Langley's observation that if the driver were not paying strict attention to the signals he could react subconsciously to the 'ready to start' indication. He went on to say that at the time of drafting a new Rule Book in 1966 (which was finally published in 1972 and is the one now in use) the Railway Inspectorate had suggested to the British Railways Board that the new Rules should place a definite duty on guards to observe starting signals where it was physically possible to do so, and not to signal to the driver to start if the platform starting signal was at Danger. The Board had considered this suggestion but had concluded that such a change would weaken the clear and

undivided responsibility placed on drivers to observe signals, and might lead to dangerous misunderstandings between drivers and guards. It was agreed, however, that the wording of the revised Rule should make it quite clear that the guard's signal to the driver meant only that the train was *ready* to start, and that it was then up to the driver to make sure that the platform starting signal was clear before actually moving off. This might be thought to be a mere tinkering with words and it is doubtful if many people noticed the different wording, let alone understood the implications of the change. It is no use the writer of the Rule understanding the subtleties of his wording if the staff who have to carry out the Rules do not understand such subtle changes.

There were 17 cases in 1972 in which drivers passed platform starting signals at Danger after receiving the 'rightaway' and Maj Rose discussed yet again with the Board the question of a Rule change, but he was eventually persuaded that it was in the interests of safety to preserve the unequivocal responsibility placed on drivers to observe and comply with signals. More accidents followed — at

Right:
A prewar scheme which was postponed. Mr Alfred Barnes, the Minister of Transport, at the controls of the first electric train from Liverpool Street to Shenfield in 1949. The LNER provided sliding-door stock for this busy suburban route.
Ian Allan Library

Staines on 4 April 1974, at Pollokshields East, Glasgow, on 11 June 1974, at Inverness on 5 September 1975 and at Wimbledon on 11 December 1976. Finally there was the crash at Paisley on Easter Monday 1979, the cause being yet again 'Ding-ding, and away'. Once more the question of what to do arose. There was still a majority within railway circles strongly opposed to changing the Rules for the reasons already given, but there was also a strong minority who felt something had to be done and that the theory that divided responsibility for the observation of signals may cause additional dangers had to be tested. What perhaps clinched the issue was the realisation during widespread investigations, of the extent to which train crews in many parts of the country (but not the Glasgow area) were already carrying out their own version of the proposed Rule change because to them it made sense not to give 'rightaway' if the platform starting signal was at Danger. In fact one driver when asked what he would do if his guard gave 'ding-ding' when the signal was still at Danger said, 'I'd ask him what the *** he thought he was playing at'. BR took the plunge and changed the Rule. The argument against the Rule change, although based on the theoretical dangers of divided responsibility, was in practice the problem of the guard not being able to see the platform starting signal in all cases. If drivers were to start relying to any extent at all on the guard not giving 'rightaway' with the signal at Danger, then a deadly trap was being laid at those places where guards could not see the signal, and it was necessary to get rid of the anomaly. A policy was therefore adopted of providing electrical indicators on platforms where they could be seen by guards and station staff and which showed when the platform starting signal was Clear by displaying an illuminated 'Off' indication. Such indicators already existed but their use was not widespread. The Rule Book alteration was a simple one — it merely told guards and station staff not to give the 'Ready to start' signal if they could see that the platform starting signal was at Danger — and it came into force on 2 February 1980. There were one or two more accidents before staff got used to the change, but it appears to have been a complete success. The fears held so strongly and for so long turned out to be groundless after all, although matters have been helped by the substantial investment in 'Off' indicators.

That the problem was mainly one of multiple-units and colour-light signals is shown by the figures for 1977 and 1978. In those two years there were 36 reported cases of platform starting signals being passed at Danger, involving 20 electric multiple-units, 11 diesel multiple-units, and only five locomotive-hauled trains. 31 cases occurred at colour-light signals and only five at semaphore signals. It is very easy to visualise the driver of a multiple-unit sitting quietly at his controls waiting for two rings on the bell, and allowing his concentration to wander, then reacting subconsciously when the rings come and setting off, forgetting about the Red signal. Indeed, drivers as a whole recognised this possibility and had a variety of home-made reminders to use in such circumstances. One driver's

63

favourite was to put his cap on the brake handle to remind him that the signal was at Red. The fact that colour-light signals were involved in so many cases may merely reflect the statistical frequency with which they are met, although because they merely differ in colour, rather than in shape as in the case of a semaphore, they may perhaps not make such an impact on a driver's mind.

Other solutions considered all involved the use of equipment at platform starting signals. The one most favoured was the installation, on the track, of an automatic warning magnet of the type used in the signalling system, a few yards beyond the signal so that the driver would be alerted by it if he were unwittingly to pass the signal at Danger, and which would have its magnetic effect suppressed when the signal was cleared. Given unlimited funds it might have been a good solution, although it might have caused problems at places where long trains had to stop with the locomotive ahead of the signal, or where the signal was placed almost at the fouling point of switch and crossing areas. Trip-stops as provided on London Transport were also considered but in addition to the considerable cost there would have been a heavy maintenance burden of equipment both at the signal and on the train. The possible use of detonator-placers, acting in conjunction with the signal, was also dismissed for similar reasons. These place a detonator on the rail when the signal is at Danger in order to alert a driver should he unwittingly pass it.

The arrangements for starting passenger trains at stations have already been shown to be less simple and more hazardous than might be supposed, but there are other dangers besides those experienced at Paisley, and they mainly concern carriage doors. The devotion shown by BR to slam-doors has long been a matter of irritation to those who have to operate the railway day by day and who would prefer sliding doors. The technology of power-operated sliding doors has been around for many years, indeed London Transport could hardly operate without it, but BR has continued to put new carriages into service with slam-doors on main-line trains, despite having experience of sliding doors over many years. For example the pre-war Southport stock of the London Midland & Scottish Railway had sliding doors, as had the postwar London & North Eastern Railway suburban stock in the Manchester area and on services from Liverpool Street. The Glasgow suburban electrification of the 1960 period was also provided with sliding door stock. All these trains were electric multiple-units, but despite that the London Midland Region reverted to slam-doors for its suburban electrification schemes introduced in the 1960s. The Southern Region too remained firmly wedded to slam-doors for many years. However, sliding doors have now been adopted as standard for suburban trains, both diesel and electric, and the new Mk 4 main-line coaches will have power-operated sliding plug-doors.

Power-operated doors make station operations much safer and help to achieve punctual departures. They are much to be preferred where there are no ticket barriers to prevent passengers from joining at the last moment just as the train is about to depart, and the trend towards 'open' stations reinforces the need for sliding doors. Fewer platform staff are required — indeed none at all in many cases. The greater safety of sliding doors is an important factor — in 1985 six passengers were killed and 25 seriously injured whilst entering or leaving trains. 16 were killed and eight seriously injured by falling out of carriage doors during the journey. Even when there are no casualties, open doors on trains during a journey cause delays and may damage other trains passing. But another important factor is the ability to run sliding-door suburban trains without guards and without platform staff.

So far as main-line coaches are concerned, BR's adherence to slam-doors is odd when one sees the extent to which power-operated doors are used on the continent, for instance on the superb SNCF Corail stock. On BR, passengers have to lower the windows to reach outside for the door handles, and then they often leave the windows open, wasting heating and air-conditioning. Frequently, even in the coldest weather, express trains are to be seen leaving stations with half their windows open, causing a gale to blow through the vestibules when the trains gain speed. BR's Mk 3 main-line coaches are so good that it is a pity they are spoilt by archaic door design, but there are signs that a more enlightened attitude is prevailing as power-operated doors are to be provided on new main-line coaches, and one hopes that retrospective action may one day be taken on High Speed Trains (HSTs).

After the 'ready to start' signal has been given to the driver there remains one problem with slam door trains — that of the passenger who attempts to join, or alight from, the train as it starts to move.

Attempting to join
The passenger who arrives on the platform just as the train is about to depart:
1 May not be aware that the 'ready to start' signal has been given. He may think that he has plenty of time to join the train and be caught unawares when it starts to move.
2 May already be aware that the 'ready to start' has been given and take a chance on being able to get safely aboard the train before it starts to move.
3 May arrive just as the train starts to move, and attempt to join it, risking the obvious dangers.

Attempting to alight
Most passengers are already standing at the carriage door as the train comes to a stop, often with the door already slightly open, and occasionally with it wide open (a thoughtless action which endangers passengers waiting on the platform if they are near the edge and not keeping a lookout). Danger often arises when passengers find they are unable to open a door for some reason — perhaps the window is stiff, or the spring of the inside handle is too strong, or the door is slightly jammed (a recurring problem on older stock) — and they then have to move down the carriage to another door, possibly encumbered with luggage and small children whilst doing so. By the time they reach it the driver may already have received the 'ready to start' signal and be preparing to move off, whereupon the situation becomes fraught with danger.

Guards and platform staff need to be aware of, and on the alert for, any of these happenings so that they can call out to anyone attempting to join or alight when it is not safe to do so, and to stop the train if necessary. Reductions in

Above right:
Incredibly the London Midland Region reverted to slam-doors on the suburban stock for their West Coast main line electrification. Here Class 304 Unit No 003 is seen on introduction to service. British Railways

Right:
It is a pity that the great Sir Herbert Walker did not specify sliding door stock on the Southern Railway. The slam-door tradition persisted long after it should have done. Here a train of 10 coaches (a 2-SAP unit leading a 4-VEP and a 4-CIG) and countless doors leaves Weybridge on a Waterloo-Haslemere train in 1979. Les Bertram

platform staff have reduced such surveillance and made it even more essential for the guard to keep a sharp lookout as the train is leaving a station, so that he can apply the brake if necessary. Where platforms are closed off by ticket barriers there is a control over late-arriving passengers but the trend now is towards open platforms. There are very good marketing reasons for removing ticket barriers — stations have a much pleasanter environment without them, and queues, congestion and delay become things of the past, but there are obvious operating and safety penalties. King's Cross has long been an example of this, where platforms 1-7 have barriers but platform 8 is open. Starting a train from platform 8 needs much more care but the environment is pleasanter for passengers. Sliding doors under the control of the driver or guard solve all these problems.

Having examined some of the many and varied aspects of safety at passenger stations, there remains the question of whether the actions of BR after the Paisley accident were appropriate and effective and, if so, why were they not implemented before the accident instead of after it? That they were effective has been proved by experience, so why were they not adopted *before* the accident? It is sad but true that it so often takes a major accident to force a change that has been resisted up to then following minor accidents or infrequent ones. Many examples could be quoted from the

Right:
A pair of Class 313 EMUs leaves Hadley Wood on a Moorgate-Welwyn Garden City train in 1979.
Brian Morrison

Below:
Modernisation at last on the Southern. Although there were problems with the Class 508s, the doors at least were an improvement. A Waterloo-Dorking train is seen leaving Wimbledon in July 1984. David Brown

long years of the history of railway accidents going back to Armagh and beyond. The Armagh accident in 1889 assisted the passage of legislation compelling railways to adopt continuous brakes on passenger trains and the block signalling system on passenger lines, in the Regulation of Railways Act of the same year. It is interesting to note in passing that the 1889 Act marked a rare example of railway safety being enforced by legislation. Practically all the advances in the safety of train operation made before and since by Government agency have been achieved by persuasion. The Hawes Junction and Ais Gill collisions of Christmas Eve 1910 and September 1913 respectively hastened the end of gas-lit coaches and brought about the more widespread use of track circuits (an electrical device which detects the presence of a train or vehicle). And the fearful double collision at Harrow & Wealdstone on 8 October 1952 led to the British Transport Commission adopting the Automatic Warning System more quickly than would otherwise have been the case. If it seems like closing the stable door after the horse has bolted one can only point to the same situation arising not only in all forms of transport, but in industry in general. It takes a serious accident or a spate of accidents to mould opinion, both public and professional, and provide a mood, an impetus, and a pressure to seek improvements and to spend money on them. Without such backing it is much more difficult to achieve improvements by persuasion.

But to return to the Paisley accident; over the many years in which a change in the Rules had been resisted there had been a gradual change in circumstances. Semaphore signals had been replaced by colour-lights at some stations, the 'sighting' of signals by guards and platform staff had been gradually improving whilst 'R' and 'Off' indicators had been installed in large numbers. The change when it came was more acceptable, but it might also be argued that it was only the railway's built-in resistance to change that prevented it from being made earlier, and that the Paisley accident was really the result of BR's refusal to act sooner, and the Railway Inspectorate's failure to press home its views more forcibly over a period of 20 years and more.

Above:
Door (and window) problems on an HST before departure at King's Cross. Author

Left:
No door problems on these superb SNCF coaches. They have power-operated fold-back doors, which can be controlled throughout the train from any door.
Ian Allan Library

Block Sections and Track Circuits

The early part of December 1981 was very wintry in the south of England. There were exceptionally low temperatures and almost a foot of snow fell. Trees hung low under its weight and the Home Counties looked more like Switzerland than England. It was all very picturesque.

On the morning of Friday 11 December 1981 the driver of the 06.03 stopping passenger train from Marylebone to High Wycombe was passing through the cutting between Gerrards Cross and Seer Green stations when he noticed that trees weighed down with snow were leaning towards the track, and he thought that the train had struck one of them. He reported the facts to the signalman at the next signalbox, High Wycombe, and advised the signalman that he should warn drivers of following trains to proceed cautiously on the line he had just travelled over. The signalman at High Wycombe telephoned his colleague at West Ruislip, which was the next signalbox open towards Marylebone, and passed on the information he had received from the driver.

After a number of trains had travelled through to High Wycombe at caution, the next train to travel over the affected line was an empty DMU and, in accordance with the Rules, the driver was stopped by the signalman at West Ruislip. Here, the signalman told the driver what had happened and that he was to proceed with extreme caution. However, approaching Gerrards Cross station, between West Ruislip and High Wycombe, the train was signalled into the platform loop line and was brought to a stand by the Home signal being at Danger. The signalman there had just arrived on duty, having been delayed by the snow; he cleared the Home signal for the train to pass it, then held a red flag out of the signalbox window as an indication to the driver that the signalman wanted to speak to him. The driver stopped his train opposite the signalbox window, and the signalman told him that the driver of the previous train through the section had reported striking a tree, and

that he was to proceed at extreme caution, to examine the track, and to report any obstruction.

The train set off slowly into the driving snow, but when it reached the cutting the driver saw the top four or five feet of a tree lying across the track. He stopped the train safely and went to a nearby railway telephone to tell the signalman at High Wycombe about the tree. He said he would be able to move it within about five minutes and went to the Guard's compartment to get an axe and a saw from the emergency toolbox.

Meanwhile the signalman at Gerrards Cross signalbox, after sending the empty DMU into the section at caution, accepted the following train, the 07.31 Marylebone-Banbury DMU, from West Ruislip signalbox, and it arrived at Gerrards Cross station within a few minutes. The signalman repeated his procedure. He kept the Home signal at Danger until the driver stopped there and sounded his horn, then he cleared the signal and stopped the train at his signalbox by holding out a red flag. As with the previous train he told the driver that there had been reports of trees down near Seer Green station and that he was to proceed cautiously. The signalman told the driver that he would clear the Starting signal (No 27) but when he tried to do so the lever would not move. The signalling arrangements between Gerrards Cross and High Wycombe signalboxes are rather unusual. There are several track circuits, and additional signals, details of which will be explained later in this chapter, but suffice it for the moment to say that if a train was standing on the track circuit in Seer Green cutting, as the empty DMU was, it would electrically lock the Starting signal at Danger. The signalman at Gerrards Cross would not have been able to clear his Starting signal for another train until the previous one had passed well clear of Seer Green cutting and the station.

The signalman looked at his track indication panel (a large diagrammatic representation of the track and signals

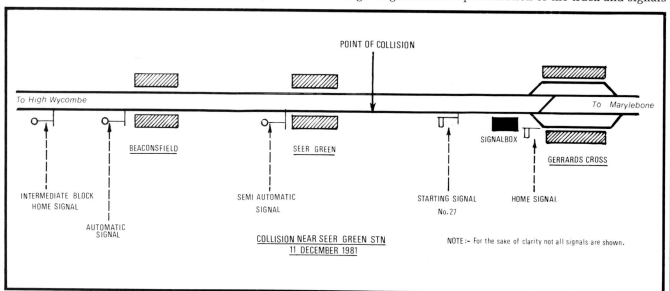

POINT OF COLLISION

To High Wycombe
To Marylebone

SIGNALBOX

BEACONSFIELD
SEER GREEN
GERRARDS CROSS

INTERMEDIATE BLOCK HOME SIGNAL
SEMI AUTOMATIC SIGNAL
STARTING SIGNAL No.27
HOME SIGNAL

AUTOMATIC SIGNAL

COLLISION NEAR SEER GREEN STN
11 DECEMBER 1981

NOTE :- For the sake of clarity not all signals are shown.

in his area). The track circuit lights at or near Seer Green station were illuminated (denoting occupied), but in addition he thought that one of the pairs of lights indicating a track circuit towards Beaconsfield (further towards High Wycombe) was also lit. It did not occur to him that the Starting signal lever might be held by the electric lock and he assumed it must be frozen. At the same time he concluded that the continuing illumination of the track circuit in Seer Green cutting must be due to a failure of the track circuit to clear behind the empty DMU, possibly due to branches brought down by it which were now lying across the rails.

Thus was the scene set for tragedy. The track circuit was correctly showing 'Occupied' because the empty DMU was standing on it in the cutting. However, the signalman told the driver that he had a track circuit failure and that he would authorise him to pass signal No 27 (the Starting signal) at Danger. He mentioned the empty DMU and the driver asked where this train was, receiving the reply that it was running down towards Beaconsfield. The signalman, in

view of what he thought was a track circuit failure, and the possibility that it was due to some obstruction, advised the driver to proceed at extreme caution, and suggested a speed of between 10 and 20mph. It seemed to the signalman that the driver was anxious to get on as he had made remarks about running late and not wanting to mess around any longer.

The train then started. The signalman closed the window and looked at his track circuit indicators. The track circuit near Beaconsfield that he had thought had been illuminated was out, and only the indicator for the track circuit at Seer Green cutting was showing 'Occupied'. Realising in a flash that something was wrong he rushed back to the window just as the second of the four coaches in the train was passing, and tried to attract attention by shouting, but no one heard him and the train disappeared into the swirling snow. The feelings of the signalman can be imagined as the full horror of what he had done came home to him. What could he do but wait helplessly, and hope. All need not be lost, he must have told himself; after all, he had told the

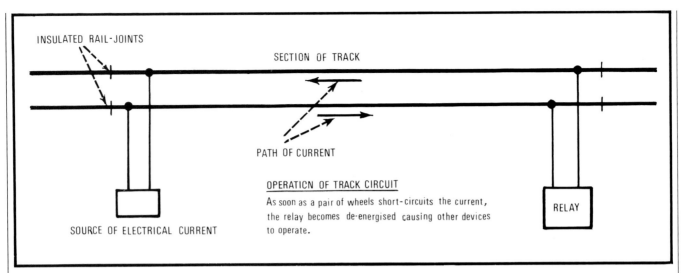

INSULATED RAIL-JOINTS

SECTION OF TRACK

PATH OF CURRENT

OPERATION OF TRACK CIRCUIT
As soon as a pair of wheels short-circuits the current, the relay becomes de-energised causing other devices to operate.

SOURCE OF ELECTRICAL CURRENT

RELAY

driver to proceed at extreme caution, so surely he would stop before running into the stationary DMU. Or maybe the driver of the stationary DMU would have removed whatever it was that was delaying him, and would have set off out of harm's way.

The signalman had not long to wait. Within a very few minutes he heard the telephone ring. With heart pounding, he answered it. His worst fears were realised — the two trains had crashed. The leading coach of the second train had partly telescoped underneath the last coach of the standing train, killing the driver, two schoolboys and a young man of 17. Five people were injured and taken to hospital.

Below:
An insulated rail-joint, as used at the end of a track circuit, or separating two adjoining track circuits.
Author/Ian Allan Library

It might be appropriate at this stage to say a few words about track circuits. They perform their allotted task not merely by telling the signalman whether there is a train on a particular piece of line, but in other ways also. When a track circuit shows 'Occupied' on the signalbox indicator, it can also:

1 put a signal to Caution or Danger behind the train,
2 electrically lock at Danger the Stop signal behind the train,
3 electrically lock a pair of facing points that the train is just approaching, so that the points cannot move dangerously. (NB facing points are those which can alter the route of an approaching train. When a train passes through them in the opposite direction they become known as trailing points),
4 indicate that a length of rail has broken (by the interruption of the current passing through it),
5 be caused by an obstruction (provided that the obstruction short-circuits the electric current),
6 indicate that a track-circuit operating clip may have been used in an emergency.

Items **1-3** are routine, and operate for every train that passes. Items **4-6** may happen without a train being present.

What is the signalman to do if a track-circuit indicator in his box continues to show 'Occupied' after a train is thought to have gone, or suddenly shows 'Occupied' when there is no train on that line? Either the track circuit is doing its proper job and is warning the signalman that there is something amiss, or else there is a fault in the equipment itself, which, being designed to fail-safe, causes the indicator to show 'Occupied'. The signalman is not to know which it is, but for safety's sake he must assume the worst. If a signalman sees a track-circuit indicator showing 'Occupied' when he would not expect it to be, he must not assume that there is a fault in the equipment but must send someone to see if there is a train or obstruction on the track. This is normally done by asking the driver of the next train requiring to go through the section to do so cautiously to see what, if anything, is amiss. If nothing is found, it can then be assumed that there is a fault, but trains must still be 'cautioned through' because the signalman will have lost the assurance given by a working track circuit. Signalling equipment is complex and varied, and the instructions to signalmen and others as to what to do in various circumstances including failure and repairs are correspondingly complex. This is particularly the case with track circuits, because of their many vital control functions.

The signalling arrangements at Gerrards Cross signalbox were more complicated than usual, and in order to appreciate this it is necessary to describe the signalling systems between Gerrards Cross and High Wycombe in some detail.

The normal signalling system between two signalboxes, the Absolute Block system, is described in an earlier chapter, but between Gerrards Cross and High Wycombe signalboxes there were two more systems, known as an automatic section and an intermediate block section respectively. These arrangements increase the number of trains that can be run over a particular line between two signalboxes (the line capacity) by, in effect, creating artificial sections without having to go to the expense of building new signalboxes and paying signalmen to operate them. More frequently they result from economy schemes where it is desired to do away with a signalbox which is no longer needed to work points leading to sidings or a branch line, the sidings or branch line having closed. If the abolition of a signalbox in such circumstances would result in such a long block section that line capacity would be reduced to an unacceptable level, it is necessary to have some means of splitting the section. There are two ways of doing this:

1 Automatic Section
Take three signalboxes, namely A, B and C. Suppose that signalbox B is to be abolished. The line between A and C could then be track-circuited throughout, and be supervised by the signalman at A, who will have track circuit indicators or a diagrammatic panel to tell him if there are any trains in the section, and roughly whereabouts. An

electrically-operated signal, probably a colour-light, will be erected about half-way and will work automatically. It will clear to green when all the track circuits beyond it are clear, and will go to red as soon as a train passes it. The signal will have its own Distant signal. The signalman at A will not offer trains to C; he will merely tell him that a train is coming, and what type (or class) it is. Where traffic density demands it, additional automatic sections may be created; there were two between Gerrards Cross and High Wycombe. In a large power signalbox area there may be dozens, or even hundreds of automatic sections, all supervised from the same signalbox.

2 Intermediate Block Sections
The cost of installing track circuits is high, and where the potential savings or other benefits of a scheme do not justify the cost of an automatic section, the Intermediate Block system provides a cheaper alternative. Take the three signalboxes A, B and C again. B is to be abolished. An additional signal will then be erected roughly mid-way between A and C, and track circuits will be installed from signalbox A to the new signal (plus an overlap for safety). As soon as a train proceeding from A to C has cleared all those track circuits the signalman at A will be able to clear his Starting signal to allow a second train to proceed towards the new signal (known as an Intermediate Block Home signal). This signal will have its own Distant signal. Any new signals of this type erected today are likely to be of the colour-light type, but existing ones may be semaphore, with the signal arm being worked by an electric motor. The section between the Intermediate Block Home signal and signalbox C will be worked in the conventional way by the offering and acceptance of trains, because it is not track-circuited. Track circuits are necessary to prove that a train has passed safely through a section, and in addition has not accidentally left part of itself behind (not an uncommon occurrence at one time with loose-coupled trains which were not braked throughout the length of the

Below & below right:
All done by magic. A means of separating track circuits from each other in continuously welded rails, known as 'Aster' track circuits. British Railways

train, and not totally unknown with supposedly fully-braked trains).

Gerrards Cross had two Automatic sections and an Intermediate Block section between that signalbox and High Wycombe, a most unusual arrangement, and it might be supposed that signalmen appointed to be in charge there would have a fair degree of seniority and experience. That would certainly have been the case in years gone by, but it was not so at the time of the accident. When a vacancy arose at Gerrards Cross it was advertised internally to those railway staff eligible to apply for it but no one applied. Consequently approaches were made to Job Centres, because the vacancy had to be filled somehow. The man recruited in this way had only taken charge in the signalbox on his own on 10 November, less than five weeks before the accident. Maj Rose, who held a Public Inquiry into this accident, considered that:

'Even with additional training, I doubt whether a new signalman, even one as intelligent as this signalman, and however competent he appeared to be, would have gained sufficient experience to take charge of a signalbox such as Gerrards Cross after only some 20 weeks of railway service. "Experience" is difficult to define but it includes the kind of general knowledge of and feel for the railway environment...'.

The railways are in a quandary in this matter, and have been ever since the last war. They have never been able to obtain enough recruits from within their own ranks for such responsible jobs as signalmen and guards; consequently they had to have recourse to Job Centres. From 1945 until the late 1970s, when the labour market was overheated, it was often very difficult to obtain suitable recruits and the turnover was high. Standards inevitably slipped a little, although rarely sufficiently to imperil safety.

In the hierarchy of railway seniority, signalmen's posts are well above the normal starting grade of railman, so why has it been so difficult to fill vacancies from among existing railwaymen? The reasons are mainly pay (or, more accurately, 'earnings potential'), and conditions of work. Gerrards Cross signalbox was closed on nights and at weekends, therefore its earnings potential was low and it was consequently unpopular. Stability of employment was another factor. Signalling was, at one time, regarded as a long-term career, but the closure of lines, sidings, stations, etc, coupled with the modernisation of signalling which puts large areas under the control of one modern power signalbox, has led to the closure of thousands of signalboxes. A young man contemplating a career as a signalman is bound to wonder just how secure his future is, because the process of abolishing old signalboxes will continue.

It will be recalled that the driver of the 07.31 Marylebone-Banbury DMU was told by the signalman at Gerrards Cross to pass signal No 27, his Starting signal, at Danger. This is obviously a vital matter and firm instructions are given in the Rule Book to both signalmen and drivers as to the circumstances in which such signals may be passed at Danger, to allow the train to enter what, in effect, then becomes No Man's Land. The main instances are:

1 A locomotive (or train) going to the assistance of a disabled train.
2 When the signal is out of order.
3 When a failure of other equipment locks the signal at Danger.
4 When single-line working is in operation (a method of working both Up and Down trains over one line, while the other line is being repaired or is obstructed).
5 During a failure of Block Instruments.
6 When a locomotive (or train) has to be used to enable the line to be examined.
7 In connection with trains which have become divided in running, or have run away.
8 When an intermediate signalbox fails to open when it should.
9 In connection with work on the line by the Engineering departments.

The philosophy of keeping the Starting signal at Danger, and instructing drivers to pass it, is to instil in them the seriousness of the situation and to remind them that there is no guarantee that the section ahead is clear, also of the need to travel very cautiously; but in most cases nowadays the signal would be electrically locked anyway and could not be cleared by the signalman. One of the most common causes of signals having to be passed at Danger is a failure

Settle Junction Up Intermediate Block Home Signal, identified as such by the white plate bearing a vertical black band halfway up the signal post. Note the telephone near the foot of the post (see close-up), enabling the driver to speak to the signalman. If the signal is at Danger and the telephone has failed, the driver is allowed to take his train forward cautiously. Author

of equipment, which is why it is understandable that a signalman might assume that a failure has happened when he finds he cannot clear a signal, although in reality the equipment is doing its proper job.

We are now left with the conundrum of why the driver of the 07.31 Marylebone-Banbury travelled so fast that he was unable to stop in time to avoid a collision with the stationary empty DMU. He may have been led to believe that the empty DMU was further away than it actually was, but according to the signalman's evidence the driver had been instructed by him to proceed at extreme caution. However, it seems that his speed in the driving snow was not less than 35mph, which, in the view of the Inspecting officer, was excessive. Had he been driving his train with the required degree of caution in the particular circumstances of reduced visibility the collision might have been avoided or its effects much reduced.

Through the years there have been several cases of accidents caused by drivers travelling too fast after having been cautioned by the signalman. On Friday 2 January 1976 high winds swept the Midlands with considerable force and many lines were blocked by fallen trees. On the line between Droitwich Spa and Worcester the winds had also brought down the telegraph poles, severing all communication between the signalboxes at Droitwich Spa and Worcester Tunnel Junction. When this happens, trains have to be worked over the line by a Time-Interval system, the instructions for which at the time were as follows:

1 To the Signalman
A train must not be allowed to pass a signalbox into the section where the failure exists without having been previously brought to a stand and the driver advised of the failure. He must also be told that Time Interval working is in operation, and then instructed by the signalman to pass

at Danger the section signal (another name for the Starting signal) and to proceed cautiously.

A train must not be allowed to proceed until the time usually taken by the preceding train to clear the section, plus an allowance for the train having been stopped and having run at caution, has elapsed. In no case, however, must a train be allowed to proceed with a lesser interval than six minutes unless the signalman can clearly see that the block section concerned is clear throughout. Where there is a tunnel in the section, an interval of not less than 10 minutes must be allowed between two trains unless the signalman can satisfy himself that the tunnel is clear.

2 To the Driver

When informed by the signalman that the block apparatus has failed, the driver will be verbally instructed to pass the section signal at Danger and he must then proceed cautiously as there may be an obstruction on the line or the section may be occupied. If, having proceeded into a section where the block apparatus has failed, the driver finds the signals for the signalbox ahead in the Clear position, he must not assume that the line is clear for his train. (Note this last requirement — it is significant.)

The section between Droitwich Spa and Worcester Tunnel Junction signalboxes is nearly 5½ miles long. A number of trains had passed in both directions under the Time Interval system on Saturday 3 January 1976, when the 05.30 train from Birmingham Curzon Street to Worcester Shrub Hill, consisting of a diesel-electric locomotive No 31241 and one parcels van, arrived at Droitwich Spa signalbox at 09.04. The signalman gave appropriate instructions to the driver, including permission to pass the Starting signal at Danger, and the train set off at 09.08. It passed through the section and arrived at the Home signal for Worcester Tunnel Junction signalbox at 09.23. There is a short tunnel between the Home signal and the signalbox and there is a telephone at the signal so that the driver and signalman can speak to each other if necessary. The signalman already knew that there was a train in the section because he had seen the track circuit showing Occupied, but as he did not know what train it was he had to wait until the driver announced himself on the telephone before he could set the appropriate route at the junction.

Meanwhile, back at Droitwich Spa a light locomotive (ie a locomotive without a train), Class 52 'Western' diesel-hydraulic No 1055 *Western Advocate*, travelling from Bescot to Gloucester, had arrived at the signalbox at 09.13. In his evidence at the Public Inquiry held by Maj King, the signalman said that he thought he had told the driver: 'The block instruments and the bells are out of order between Droitwich and Tunnel Junction. There is no telephone communication: all the telephones are out of order. We are working on the Time Interval system, and will you proceed cautiously through the section, and pass Signal 70 [the Starting signal] at Danger . . . I shall have to keep you for a minute or two until a suitable time has elapsed'.

The light locomotive departed at 09.18, 10 minutes after the parcels train, which was still in the section. Normally, to have two trains in a section at the same time is a situation that signalmen dread — the first words in the Absolute Block Signalling Regulations say that the object of the system is to prevent more than one train being in a block section on the same line at the same time. Nevertheless there should have been no danger — the weather was fine and clear, it was daylight, and the driver of the light engine had been well appraised of the circumstances. He was fully experienced with many years' service, and knew that he had to keep a sharp lookout as there was no guarantee that the section was clear. Indeed,

the special Time Interval method of working implicitly assumes that a second train might enter a section before the train in front has passed completely through it. More than that, it assumes that as individual drivers may drive at different speeds while passing through the section (one train may have a better brake, another a heavier load) a second train might catch up with the one in front whilst they are both still on the move. It also assumes the possibility that the first train might have stopped out of course for some reason (eg a breakdown) anywhere in mid-section. There should be no danger, provided that the second driver is travelling with the necessary degree of care, and can stop within the distance ahead that he can see the line to be clear.

Meanwhile, at the parcels train standing at the Home signal at Worcester Tunnel Junction the driver walked back from the telephone and climbed aboard his locomotive, little knowing that approaching him at fairly high speed, and getting closer all the time, was the light locomotive. Seeing the signal at Clear, he sat down and released the brake valve and was waiting for the brakes to come off when he suddenly felt a tremendous thump. No 1055 had crashed into the back of him at about 45mph, killing its driver, and the guard who was riding with him. The time was 09.25.

We shall never know why the light locomotive was going so fast. It had come through the 5½-mile section in approximately seven minutes, and Maj King concluded that it was not being driven with the caution that the circumstances demanded. The Home signal at Tunnel Junction (but not the Distant) was cleared as No 1055 approached it; in fact the driver may have seen the signal arm move from Danger to Clear, but the Rule warned him that he should not assume that the line was clear for *his* train. Did the Clear signal lead him into a trap? We shall never know. It is a warning which was inserted in the Rules as long ago as 1924 specifically to draw drivers' attention to the possibility of such a trap.

This accident demonstrates how great a part that fate sometimes plays. If No 1055 had approached Worcester Tunnel Junction a minute earlier the Home signal might still have been at Danger and the driver would, unless something very unusual had happened, have slowed down in time to stop at it (and avoided colliding with the very short train in front). A minute later, and the signal might already have been put back to Danger behind the parcels train before it was seen by the driver of No 1055.

An accident similar in some ways to the one at Seer Green occurred at Hyndland on the North Glasgow electrified line, on 5 June 1980. Fortunately there were no fatalities, although 35 passengers and three members of the traincrews had to be taken to hospital. The line concerned is track-circuited throughout, and has colour-light signals and AWS. There had been an earlier failure of signalling equipment and the train service had been disrupted. During the morning the signalman noticed a track circuit showing 'Occupied' although he could not remember a train being there, so he asked the driver on the opposite line to have a look as he went past. Unfortunately there was a misunderstanding between them and the driver reported that the line was clear. Satisfied that the occupation of the track circuit was due to a fault in the equipment and not to the presence of a train, the signalman authorised the driver of the 09.27 Dalmuir-Motherwell passenger train, a three-coach electric multiple-unit, to pass the protecting colour-light signal at Danger. In his evidence at the Public Inquiry the signalman said that he had told the driver that there was a track circuit failure ahead and that he was to proceed with caution, although this was disputed by the driver, who said that he was not instructed to proceed with

caution nor was he told why it was necessary for the signal to be passed at Danger. The driver accelerated his train to between 25 and 30mph even though his forward visibility was severely limited by the curvature of the line, and he was thus unable to prevent his train from colliding violently with a train that was standing on the track circuit, another three-coach electric multiple-unit which was empty and which was waiting to set back into the maintenance depot. Maj Rose, who held a Public Inquiry into the collision, concluded that the driver had failed to drive his train with the necessary caution after being told to pass a signal at Danger and that the signalman had too readily assumed that the 'Occupied' indication of the track circuit was due to a failure of the equipment rather than the presence of a train. Maj Rose also commented on a general laxity in passing verbal messages concerning train movements and the safety of the line.

We have met the 22.15 sleeping car express from King's Cross to Edinburgh before, when it was derailed at Lincoln in 1961, and we are about to meet it again. During the night of Saturday 7 November 1981, trains which normally ran on the East Coast main line from King's Cross were having a lengthy diversion over the Midland main line north of Sheffield because of engineering work. At Altofts Junction, between Normanton and Leeds, the routes diverge, the Midland main line continuing to Leeds, and the other line proceeding to York. The diverted trains were using the latter to regain their booked route. The 21.00 King's Cross-Edinburgh express had been sent to the Starting signal at Altofts Junction and was held there for some time by the signalman who then apparently forgot about it and assumed that the track circuit, which was indicating the presence of the train, had failed. When the 22.15 sleeper from King's Cross arrived at his signalbox he authorised the driver to pass his Home signal at Danger, as it was electrically locked and he could not clear it. The driver of the sleeping car express took his train forward and collided at a speed of between 10 and 15mph with the rear of the express standing at the Starting signal, slightly injuring seven passengers. The young signalman had worked at

Altofts Junction signalbox for only 2½ months. This accident contained a number of familiar features:

1 The signalman assumed that a track circuit had failed when in reality it was doing its proper job.
2 Was the driver of the second train misled into thinking the line was clear?
3 The rear of the first train was not sufficiently conspicuous to prevent the second train from crashing into it.
4 The relative inexperience of the signalman.

As a result of these accidents and others of a similar nature BR considered what more could be done. The problem was not becoming less frequent, and is not likely to become so in the future. As more and more equipment which has a safety function is provided in signalboxes and in the signalling system, it is only to be expected that the total number of failures might increase, even if the failure rate per item of equipment remains constant. In order to be able to keep trains running during a failure the signalman has to resort to special alternative measures and these very often require drivers to pass signals at Danger. It is very easy for the signalman to assume that, when something unforeseen occurs, it is due to technical failure, rather than the particular piece of equipment doing the job for which it was designed, which is guarding the safety of trains and protecting passengers against the possible effects of failure of the human element.

The importance of avoiding delays to trains, and of maintaining high standards of punctuality and reliability, are constantly being drummed into signalmen, and these are indeed very important issues, but there is a risk, no matter how slight, that constant emphasis on standards of service to the customer may assume an importance greater than it ought to vis-à-vis safety. Safety must always be paramount, but at the same time the conscientious signalman or driver is always anxious to minimise delays, hence the occasional lapse, which is often not the result of recklessness or carelessness, but is the result of a genuine concern to do one's best for the customer, part of the railway tradition of service.

BR's considerations were based on two possibilities — (1) the issuing of a printed notice to a driver by the signalman whenever a signal has to be passed at Danger, and (2) the laying down of a maximum speed at which a driver may travel after passing a signal at Danger. The advantages of the printed notice, or ticket, were thought to be as follows:

1 The completion of a ticket would give the signalman a breathing space in which to collect his thoughts.
2 The ticket would specify which signal was to be passed at Danger, and the reason, eg signal locked at Danger by track circuit showing Occupied.
3 The ticket could carry a warning to the driver reminding him of the need to travel cautiously, prepared to stop short of any obstruction, and pointing out that there may well be a train or other obstruction anywhere on the line ahead.
4 If it were decided to impose maximum speeds this could be shown on the ticket.
5 It would reduce the risk of misunderstanding which is always present with messages passed by word of mouth, especially on the telephone.
6 It would provide the driver with a record of being authorised to pass a signal at Danger, in case of subsequent dispute.

Both drivers and signalmen would be supplied with tear-off booklets of tickets. Where the message is given verbally, the signalman would complete a ticket and hand it to the driver; where the message is given over the telephone the driver would complete the ticket. This procedure is followed on some Continental railways but it was finally concluded by BR that the situation was not sufficiently serious to justify such a change. However, the idea is available should the position deteriorate. It was argued that the driver might find it difficult to complete a ticket standing at a lineside telephone in the dark and in pouring rain, but the answer to that objection is that if the driver can't remember what he has been told when he gets back to the warmth and light of his cab, to complete the ticket there, he isn't in a position to take his train forward safely. What is certain is that some drivers would have welcomed the ticket system. They are often uneasy about passing signals at Danger in case of dispute or argument afterwards, and the existence of a ticket would be documentary proof in their favour.

The second consideration concerned the laying down of a maximum speed. It would obviously be inappropriate to lay down one specific speed, because it would have to be low enough to be safe in the worst conditions of darkness, fog, etc without imposing unnecessary delay in conditions of bright sunshine — an impracticability. There are so many factors to be taken into account:

1 Daylight or darkness.
2 Clear or foggy.
3 Curvature of the line.
4 Obstruction to the forward view caused by overbridges, station buildings, etc.
5 Tunnels and their length.
6 Severity of gradient, rising or falling.
7 Effectiveness of available brake-power.

Many of the factors may not be constant throughout a long section. Eventually, after much debate, two alternatives emerged; to lay down maximum speeds of 30mph for clear weather in daylight and 15/20mph in darkness or poor visibility, leaving the driver to use his judgement to run at a lower speed if conditions required it. The other alternative was not to quote specific maximum speeds in case they came to be regarded as the norm, but to leave it to drivers' judgement, whilst at the same time drawing their attention to the problem. The second alternative was chosen and a notice to drivers was issued to be kept at the front of one of the books of Rules and Regulations known as the *General Appendix to Working Timetables and Books of Rules and Regulations*. It is a sort of all-purpose volume for those instructions which do not naturally fit into any of the other publications, so as a result it is quite a thick book, although vigorously weeded from time to time. The difference between the Rule Book and the General Appendix is basically that the Rule Book sets out safe procedures for running trains under varying circumstances, but without explanation; it says 'Do this' or 'Do that' and wisely leaves no room for debate or argument. The Rules, as far as possible, are clear and concise; at least that is the aim, although the complexities of modern equipment sometimes make it difficult to achieve. The *General Appendix*, on the other hand, can allow itself the luxury of explanation and amplification. The notice to drivers referred to reads as follows:

When a signalman instructs a driver to pass a signal at Danger and travel cautiously through a section . . . the Driver must travel at such a reduced speed as will enable him to stop safely and well clear of any train or other obstruction which may be on the line ahead. In determining the safe speed at which he may travel the Driver must be guided by the braking capability of his train and his view of the line ahead, due regard being paid to darkness, fog or falling snow, or where curvature of the line restricts the view of the line ahead, or any other adverse circumstances. THE DRIVER MUST ALWAYS BE ABLE TO STOP WITHIN THE DISTANCE HE CAN SEE THE LINE TO BE CLEAR.

Whether this will be sufficiently effective remains to be seen, but so far it appears to be. If events prove otherwise, BR has two shots in its locker.

There remains one more question to consider — the passing of messages by word of mouth. As we have seen, such messages can quite literally be a matter of life and death, therefore the importance of passing them accurately and understanding them fully cannot be over-emphasised, but if safety is to be assured the content of the message being passed must be right too. This means that the giver of the message must have accurately assessed the situation, avoided jumping to any wrong conclusions or making false assumptions, chosen his words carefully and phrased his message clearly, unambiguously, concisely and in accordance with the Rules. Should the message contain explanation or merely instructions? Explanations might make the message easier to understand, but they can also distract and mislead, despite the best of intentions. Speculation must be avoided, in case the seeds of a wrong assumption are planted in the recipient's mind. The environment in which messages are passed is often very unhelpful, as for example in the case of the signalman having to lean out of his signalbox window to shout a message to a driver, possibly in a dialect which is not the driver's, using local terminology, in a howling wind against the throb of a diesel engine. It is not likely to be a model of grammatical elegance, and bitter experience teaches that it may not be correctly understood. Or picture a driver speaking to a signalman from a lineside telephone; one which is located between two tracks with other trains whistling by at 100mph or more, and with rain water trickling down his neck. One can only wonder that there are not more errors.

Radio helps to overcome the environmental problems mentioned in passing messages, and by its very nature causes messages to be passed in a more disciplined manner, partly because mistakes can be made so easily if the laid-down procedures for identification, etc are not properly followed. It might also be added that if radio had been available to the signalman at Gerrards Cross he might have been able to tell the driver of the DMU to stop his train, in time to avoid the crash (see also the discussion on the Invergowrie collision in Chapter 2). It is clear that the provision of radio on a wide scale could greatly assist the cause of safety but its use on BR for communication between signalmen and drivers is coming very slowly, although early in 1986 BR ordered sufficient sets of train radio equipment from Storno Ltd to equip 525 locomotives and multiple-units, at a cost of £1 million. The cab-mounted radio-telephones will have emergency buttons to alert controllers to any hazard. Progress could be quicker, but once again it is a question of money, with the British Railways Board being increasingly squeezed year by year by the government of the day to reduce its financial support from public funds. Continental railways do not suffer from such financial hardships — the French, the Germans and the Dutch, for example, have already equipped most of their trains with radio, whilst British Rail have only just started with the suburban lines from St Pancras and King's Cross and on lines in parts of Scotland and Wales.

The attitude of the railway Trade Unions to radio on trains is interesting. Individual drivers would welcome it because they can see its advantages, and their Union, ASLEF, adopted a not unhelpful attitude. The National Union of Railwaymen on the other hand was more cautious in its approach because it could see that radio would help BR to run trains without guards, and unfortunately the two issues became linked, culminating in industrial action. The introduction of radio was delayed for several years.

The Seer Green accident was a classic of its kind because it raised so many questions. We have ranged far and wide in this chapter discussing the many issues, the most important of which were:

1 Safe procedures for authorising drivers to pass signals at Danger.
2 What to do when track circuits unexpectedly show Occupied.
3 The speed of trains after the driver has been cautioned and sent past a signal at Danger.
4 Passing verbal messages.
5 Recruiting experienced signalmen for complex signalboxes.
6 Avoiding jumping to conclusions.
7 Radio communication between drivers and signalmen.

Could an accident of the Seer Green type happen again? The answer must be that the possibility still exists, although the likelihood is remote. Most of the remedial action has consisted of amending the Rules and Regulations yet again. That is fine if every driver and every signalman reads the amendments, understands them and the reasoning behind them, and is then sufficiently well-informed and experienced to apply them correctly at a time of pressure. It is a lot to expect of the system.

What else could BR have done? It could have:

1 Made the rear of trains more conspicuous by providing two bright tail lamps on all passenger trains.
2 Provided guards with emergency flares.
3 Provided radio communication between signalmen and drivers.
4 Introduced a ticket system for passing signals at Danger.
5 Laid down maximum speeds at which trains may travel after being cautioned and passing signals at Danger.
6 Avoided having inexperienced signalmen in complicated signalboxes.
7 Provided 'refreshers' for drivers, to ensure that their Rules knowledge was always up-to-date and that, as far as possible, they understood the implications of, and the reasons for, changes in the Rules.

BR has already made considerable progress with item 1 (tail lamps), whilst item 3 (radio) is being introduced as fast as BR feel that it can be afforded. None of the other measures is particularly expensive so why has BR not adopted them? The reason can only be that the situation was judged not to be sufficiently serious to justify the changes in operating procedures involved. Would those changes prevent another accident of the Seer Green type? The answer must be that they could not be guaranteed to do so, but only that they would make another accident less likely. But let the last word rest with Maj Rose, in his report dated 31 January 1983: '(The Seer Green accident) was made more poignant by the fact that such accidents are rare events . . . In four out of the past seven years not a single passenger died in a train accident. Rail travel is now safer than it has ever been . . . I do not believe that (this accident) has indicated any area, other than the continued replacement of outworn semaphore signalling by centralised colour-light signalling, where large additional investment in safety measures would be justified or cost effective.'

7 In the Signalbox

No trains run, except in sidings, without the full knowledge and consent of the signalman. He is vitally involved in every case. One false step on his part, a wrong assumption, a hasty conclusion or just plain human forgetfulness, could lead to disaster; and has often done so in the past. Yet, of the eight Public Inquiries held by Inspecting Officers of the Department of Transport into serious accidents in 1984, none involved the signalman. Three of the accidents were caused by driver's error, three had a technical cause, one was caused by the light in a tail lamp going out and one was caused when a train ran into cattle which had strayed on to the line. In 1983 a signalman was involved in just one accident (at Wrawby Junction, Eastern Region) out of six which were the subject of Public Inquiries, and in 1982 one out of five (at Clayton Bridge level crossing, near Manchester). There has been only one case of an accident being caused by irregularities in the working of the Absolute Block Signalling system since 1977.

It is a matter of interest that both the accidents mentioned in which signalmen were involved (Wrawby Junction and Clayton Bridge) occurred during failures of signalling equipment. At Wrawby Junction the signalman overlooked the need to put a clamp on some points worked by an electric motor during a failure. The points then

Below:
The wreckage of the leading coach of the DMU involved in the collision at Wrawby Junction between the 17.32 passenger train from Cleethorpes to Sheffield and an oil-tank train on 9 December 1983. One passenger was killed. John Wright

moved unbeknown to him and caused two trains to collide. In the case of the Clayton Bridge accident, the level crossing there is operated remotely by the signalman at Baguley Fold Junction, some distance away, and monitored by him by means of closed-circuit television equipment. A track circuit had developed a technical fault and was locking a Stop signal at Danger to prevent it being cleared. This signal protected the level crossing, and the signalman authorised the driver to pass the signal at Danger. The barriers at the level crossing were already lowered across the road for a train travelling in the opposite direction and as soon as that train had cleared the crossing the barriers started to rise whilst the other train was just about to go over it. A car set off over the crossing and was hit by the train. The signalman had overlooked the fact that he had left the operating switch for the barriers in the 'automatic-raise' position, and he should have placed it in the 'manual' position before authorising the driver to pass the signal at Danger. We have noticed before how new or unfamiliar equipment can contain its own hidden hazards, especially during a failure.

When one considers the total number of trains which signalmen deal with each day, and the ever-present possibility of error, BR has a magnificent safety record, and one of which signalmen, and British Rail as a whole, can be, and are, rightly proud. Yet how has it come about?

This chapter is not intended to be a history of signalling, except perhaps for the last few years. There are other books available which cover that fascinating story. Suffice it to say that safety in signalboxes has always been the subject of close managerial and technical study ever since the

Clayton Bridge level crossing, before its conversion to remotely-controlled lifting barriers, showing '8F' 2-8-0 No 48652 on an enthusiasts' railtour on 27 May 1968. D. A. Idle

operation of points and signals was collected together locally in one signalbox in the early days of railways. Every accident is studied to see what lessons there are to be learnt, so that remedies can be applied, and although by now there is little new to discover about safety in signalboxes, changes in methods or equipment may bring new hidden dangers.

Let us look in one of the thousands of traditional manual signalboxes which still remain today to see how safety is provided for, and consider separately the signalman, the signalling equipment, the method of working, and the operating of trains. To take the signalman first. What are the qualities needed? He needs self-reliance, because he has to act on his own with very little supervision; self-discipline, to be able to accept and apply the rigid disciplines of the signalling system and the Rules; resourcefulness to cope with emergencies; self-confidence to deal with the pressures of train working and failures of equipment; and steadiness both to accept periods of inactivity between trains and to cope safely with the urgent demands of failures and emergencies. It is no mere coincidence that these are the qualities which might describe a policeman; the original railway signalmen were policemen employed by the early railways, and signalmen are still known as 'Bobbies'.

Signalmen receive very little direct supervision, nor do the better ones require it. A visit once or twice a week by the local Manager or Area Inspector is the norm, the purpose being to see that the working is strictly in accordance with the Rules and Regulations; that the equipment is in proper working order; and that the emergency equipment is in its proper place and readily available. The supervisor will also examine the train register book, in which the signalman records the time at which all bell signals are sent or received and any unusual events. The signalman is required to enter these times immediately so that he always has an up-to-the-minute record of the state of train-working. But the most important aspect of the supervision of signalmen, as with any supervision, is to know the quality of the men concerned, how reliable and dependable they are, how conscientious, how good their knowledge is and how good they are at applying it. It is important to recognise their strengths and weaknesses, so that supervision, help and guidance can be directed where it is most needed and where it will be most effective. It is particularly important to be able to spot the man who is unreliable or careless so that he can be specially watched and dealt with as necessary. It is also necessary to keep a fatherly eye on those keen young signalmen who, without the benefit of maturity gained from years of experience, may act impetuously in their anxiety to minimise delay during failures or emergencies.

Moving on now to an examination of the equipment in the traditional signalbox; the most striking feature is the row of levers which operate the points and signals. They are

79

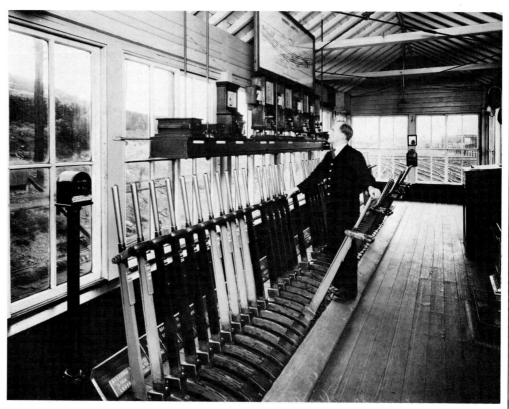

Right:
The austere and functional interior of an LNWR signalbox is well portrayed in this view of Marsden signalbox on the Huddersfield-Manchester route, taken at least 40 years ago. Although this was a busy four-track route the signalman had only the basic equipment to help him. On the 'block shelf' above the row of levers can be seen the block instruments and bells. There appears to have been no electrical control on the starting signals, which would therefore have been free to be pulled at any time. LNWR lever frames were very solidly built. British Railways

painted in different colours for the different functions and are interlocked so that they cannot be operated in confliction with each other. On a shelf above the frame of levers are the block signalling instruments, the bells for receiving signalling messages from the next signalbox and the tappers for sending them. As mentioned in Chapter 2 there are electrically-operated safety controls governing the operation of the block instruments and signals. There are also indicators of various types showing the operation of track circuits, the position of signal arms which are out of sight and whether signal lamps are lit or not. Above the shelf there is a large diagram giving the track layout of the area under the control of the signalman, with points, signals, gradients, distances, etc shown on it. In busier signalboxes some of the indicators just mentioned may be electrically incorporated in the diagram so that the signalmen can see at a glance where trains are. There will also be a supply of detonators for use in an emergency and there may be detonator-placing equipment, usually operated by a lever in the frame, which places detonators on the line opposite the signalbox to warn drivers in a last-minute emergency. Finally there will be a red flag, a green flag and a handlamp which can show separately red, green, and white.

The method of working depends on the type of line, but it is usually the Absolute Block System for double lines outside modern power-signalled areas. The use of the Block system on lines used by passenger trains represents one of the very few cases where Parliament has actually intervened to compel railway companies to adopt safety measures. Section 1 of the Regulation of Railways Act 1889 enacts that:

'The Board of Trade may from time to time order a railway company . . . to adopt the Block system on all or any of their railways open for the public conveyance of passengers.'

The system has already been described on page 29. On some lines used only by freight trains (usually known as goods lines), and often at busy passenger stations, a form of working is adopted, known as Permissive Block, which allows more than one train to be in a section at once. Speeds on such lines are low and if a train is being allowed into a section which is already occupied by another train, the driver is made aware of this by the signalman using a special signal, known as a Calling-on signal, which takes the form of a miniature arm located below the Stop signal. This type of working used to be extremely common and it was a frequent sight 20 or 30 years ago to have freight trains queuing up one behind the other on the approaches to marshalling yards, etc. Now, with changes in the pattern of freight working it is becoming much rarer.

It will readily be appreciated that allowing trains to follow each other in such a manner is not without a degree of danger, and requires the driver to keep a sharp lookout, especially during darkness. Accidents are still occurring on such lines — on 7 November 1980 the 12.10 freight train from Guide Bridge to Bayston Hill, hauled by Class 47 diesel-electric locomotive No 47190, crashed into the rear of another freight train at 25mph in daylight and good visibility on the Up Salop Goods Line at Crewe. The driver, who together with the guard was killed, was considered by the Inspecting Officer at the Public Inquiry not to have kept a good lookout, as the train in front could be seen for 200yd, yet the driver did not start to brake until he was only 60yd from it.

On 3 February 1984, at 02.14, a particularly unfortunate set of circumstances led to the death of a driver and guard at Wigan North Western station. A points failure was causing some delays, and trains were being detained at signals. A Freightliner train was standing just beyond the station at a colour-light signal worked from Warrington power signalbox. Standing at the next signal behind was Speedlink freight train 6M79, the 21.05 Mossend (Glasgow)-Bescot (Birmingham), hauled by an electric locomotive No 86032. The line through the station was authorised for permissive working when necessary, but only for passenger trains. However, the signalman, anxious to move 6M79 forward so that he could divert an express round the two freight trains, gave the driver permissive authority to draw

forward. Whilst the signalman was not specifically authorised to do this, it was not unsafe as all the signalling equipment necessary to allow it to be done safely was provided; it was merely that, due to changes in the pattern of freight train working, it was no longer necessary for freight trains to follow each other in a permissive manner at Wigan, therefore the authority to do so had been cancelled. The driver of 6M79 received the appropriate permissive signal (two small white lights, one diagonally above the other), which was located on the same post as the main line signal and a few feet below it, the main line signal remaining correctly at Red. The rear wagon of the Freightliner train was empty and its low flat profile was almost invisible. The tail lamp, which might have saved the day, was out. In the darkness and rain 6M79 ran into the back of the Freightliner train and both driver and guard were killed. No blame could be attached to the driver; what was needed was a more reliable tail lamp. This was the third collision in five years where a second train had run into the back of a Freightliner train whose tail lamp had failed.

To return to our story, however. We have looked at the signalman, his equipment and his rules. He is now ready to start signalling trains. But he needs something else if he is to do his job properly. He needs a timetable so that he knows what trains to expect, where they go to, and when. He also needs to know how to recognise them and how they rank for priority in running. All trains have an individual four-character number, the first digit being the train classification, the second a letter indicating a geographical area or destination region. The third and fourth numbers give the individual train number. All trains are grouped in classes 1-9, and 0; the classes being:

Class 1: Express passenger train
Postal train
Newspaper train
Breakdown van train going to clear the line or returning therefrom
Light locomotive going to assist disabled train or snow plough going to clear the line
Motorail train not conveying passengers

Class 2: Ordinary passenger train
Breakdown van train or snow plough not going to clear the line
Officers' special train

Class 3: Parcels train permitted to run at 90mph or over

Class 4: Freight train permitted to run at more than 60mph

Class 5: Empty coaching stock train

Class 6: Freight train not permitted to run at more than 60mph

Class 7: Freight train not permitted to run at more than 45mph

Class 8: Freight train timed at 35mph or below or conveying wagons with maximum permitted speed of 35mph

Class 9a: Freight train not fully fitted but with brake force not less than shown in Working Manual for Rail Staff

Class 9b: Unfitted freight train

Class 0: Light locomotive(s)

Notes 1   The term 'Freight Train' includes parcel trains
     2   All trains except Class 9 must be continuously braked
     3   Engineers' trains and machines will be classified by their speed
     4   The term 'Breakdown van train' includes an overhead wiring train.

Trains used to be recognisable by the arrangement of one or two white lights at the front, and every schoolboy eventually found out what the different arrangements meant, in fact every book on railways, intended for boys, contained a full set of diagrams; one lamp at each side of the buffer beam was the most exciting, because that denoted an express passenger train. This system continued until the end of the steam era, in fact the early diesels were equipped appropriately with small electric lights, and hinged white discs for daytime use.

Trains have always had their own individual numbers for identification purposes but these are only shown in the working timetables issued to the staff, and not in the public timetables. Continental railway administrations however, make widespread use of train numbers in their advertising literature and passenger information systems. When the four-character system was introduced on BR, locomotives were equipped with illuminated boxes or panels at each end so that the number could be exhibited on roller blinds for the benefit of operating staff. This was a very useful operating facility, which was particularly valuable when the service was disrupted, but the Mechanical Engineer found the blinds expensive to maintain, so the indicator boxes were blanked out. From an operating point of view it was a great pity, but it was a victim of the incessant financial pressures on BR.

Signalmen at junctions obviously need to be aware of the identity of approaching trains, and there are a number of ways of achieving this:

1 By using special 'Is line clear?' bell signals for trains going on to the branch line.

2 By using special 'train entering section' bell signals for trains going on to the branch line.
3 By the use of a special telegraph needle, deflected one way for the branch, the other way for the main line.
4 By telephone-circuiting, in which the identity of the train is either given to a number of signalboxes simultaneously; or individually after the 'Is line clear?' bell signal has been sent.

At large stations signalmen do not usually clear their signals for a train which has stopped there, until they are told that it is ready to leave, in case it is delayed for reasons unknown to the signalman. The advice to the signalman that a train is ready to leave is usually given electrically by the platform supervisor pressing a plunger or button known as a 'Train Ready to Start' button, which operates an indicator in the signalbox.

By a process of gradual improvement over many years, by the application of technical skills and ingenuity, the use of the latest techniques and much capital investment, signalling has been brought to a very high level of safety indeed. One accident which might be taken as a landmark

Left:
Train No 1E69, the 09.50 Poole-Bradford, pulling out of Leamington Spa on 14 September 1974. Station staff en route would have had no problem in identifying this train even on a busy Saturday with trains running out of sequence — the helpful train number exhibited on the locomotive saw to that. Leamington Spa is the site of British Railways' latest leap forward in signalling technology — solid-state interlocking, which replaces the use of banks of electrical relays.
Brian Morrison

deliberately adopting an irregular method of operating the Block System, by using a short-cut procedure. This saved them work; in particular it saved them from having to get up from their seats so often to answer the bells. The standard of supervision was too low, despite regular visits to the signalbox by a variety of Inspectors and Managers. To supervise effectively the supervisor needs to know the signalman's job thoroughly. He also needs to be aware of, and keep a sharp lookout for, the tell-tale signs that everything is not as it should be. However, Area Managers, their assistants and Inspectors cover large areas nowadays, which may contain many signalboxes. Some signalboxes may only be visited by a supervisor once or twice a week which means, taking the effects of shift work into account, that individual signalmen may only be seen once or twice a month, and then only for a short time. The amount of supervision that can be given in such circumstances is clearly very small. It is fortunate therefore that the great majority of signalmen work perfectly well (and safely) with such minimal supervision, but it is all the more important to be able to identify the few who do not.

In years gone by, all stations of any size had their own station masters, whilst smaller stations were paired. There was, therefore, regular on-the-spot supervision of a type that cannot be given today: indeed, the situation is getting worse, as British Rail continue to amalgamate areas, making local supervision even more remote. There is a strong case, not only on safety grounds but on commercial grounds too, for restoring station masters to the larger stations. It makes no sense at all to have such stations as Lancaster, Durham and Taunton without a resident 'Mr Railway', with the dignity and status, or what one might call the 'recognisable presence', of the former station master. The young traffic managers of today may be good at management, but 'presence' requires a certain maturity which they have not yet had time to acquire. The young signalmen at Gerrards Cross and Altofts Junction (and at Chinley, where a driver was killed in a collision in March 1986) would all have benefitted from closer and more frequent supervision. Whether the accidents would then not have happened is impossible to say, but there is at least a chance that they would not have done.

Although the Liverpool-Southport line is a busy suburban route, with trains every few minutes in the peak, the signalling equipment lacked many of the controls which one would have expected to find there, indeed there were virtually none between Hall Road signalbox and the next two signalboxes towards Southport, ie Hightown and Eccles Crossing. Yet, there had been a previous collision at Hall Road in 1961, after which Col McMullen, the Inspecting Officer, had recommended that a number of specific controls be provided to safeguard against human error or forgetfulness; whether from simple failure of the human element or arising from slack working. What Col McMullen actually said was: 'The signalmen at Hall Road . . . are required to deal with over 100 trains per day in each direction. There are, however, no block controls on the Starting signals and there is no Welwyn Control[1] . . . For traffic of this nature full track-circuiting and train

because it led to a decision to increase over BR as a whole the extent to which particular safeguards were applied, occurred on 4 July 1977 near Hall Road station on the suburban electrified line between Southport and Liverpool.

The 20.15 three-car electric train from Southport to Liverpool had been stopped for about 5min at the Home signal at Hall Road signalbox because the signal was at Danger. The signal was then cleared and the train had just started to move off when it was run into in the rear at about 20mph by a five-car electric train, the 20.30 Southport-Liverpool. All the vehicles of both trains were damaged but fortunately no one was killed, although 35 people were taken to hospital, two of whom were detained overnight.

This was a classic case of 'Two in a section', the signalman's nightmare, and it arose from irregularities in the working of the Block System by the signalman at the next signalbox open on the Southport side of Hall Road, ie Eccles Crossing, who wrongly allowed the second train to proceed, having concluded that the section was clear. The Public Inquiry, held by Maj Olver, an Inspecting Officer, brought to light a number of unsatisfactory features.

There was evidence that some signalmen were at times

describers are desirable, but this equipment is expensive. I do, however, think that at least a block release on the Starting signals and the Welwyn Control should be provided . . . and I recommend that consideration should be given to their provision.' Unfortunately BR had not implemented this recommendation, although they had already programmed the work for 1978 when the second Hall Road accident occurred.

After the second Hall Road accident BR determined to make some amends, not only on the Southport line but anywhere else where similar conditions existed[2]. They adopted the following new standards:

1 On important lines, ie main trunk routes and/or routes with 10 or more trains in the same direction in any one peak hour

(i) The Home signal lever and the Distant signal arm must be proved to be in the Normal Position (ie lever back in its frame, signal arm at Caution) before the Block Instrument can be placed at 'Line Clear'.

(ii) There must be a berth track circuit on the approach side of the Home signal which, when occupied, would place the Block Indicator to 'Train in Section', or hold it in that position. Welwyn Control must be provided.

(iii) There must be sequential interlocking between the Home and Starting signals.

(iv) The Starting signal must be electrically locked at Danger until released by the Block Indicator for the next signalbox being placed to 'Line Clear' for one operation of the signal only. A second operation must require a second 'Line Clear'.

2 On less important lines of a more local nature

The controls and equipment mentioned in 1(i) and 1(iv) must be provided.

The work was staged over a number of years because of its cost and the demands on technical manpower at a time when staff numbers were being reduced to allow BR to meet its government-imposed financial targets. Actually the capital cost of the additional equipment was not great, and could easily have been met out of one year's budget, but the work was labour-intensive and to have concentrated the limited technical resources on it would have delayed other worthwhile projects.

The term 'Welwyn Control' has been used a number of times. It denotes a piece of equipment designed after a particularly serious accident at Welwyn Garden City in 1935 and is provided in conjunction with the equipment and controls mentioned in 1(ii) above. After the Block Indicator has been placed in the 'Train in Section' position it cannot be turned to any other position until the train has

1

Contrasting Architectural Styles in Power Signalboxes

1 **Manchester Piccadilly, opened in 1960.** British Railways

2 **Coventry, dating from 1962. Light and airy, the design gives the signalmen an all-round view, a feature lacking from more recent designs.** British Railways

3 **The nadir of signalbox design? The wooden hut on the roof is not a pigeon loft but the signalling operations room. This signalbox — Reading — covers a very wide area.** British Railways

4 **An original design, to say the least. Birmingham New Street. The signalling operations room is on the top floor.** British Railways

5 **Into the 1970s. Designed to confuse a potential saboteur into thinking that it is a crematorium, or a modern waste-disposal plant? Motherwell.** British Rail

6 **The most unlikely-looking signalbox ever? This building, at Westbury, has a distinctly central-European look about it.** D. E. Conway

2

been proved to have passed through the section by its occupation of the berth track circuit at the Home signal. The question then arises of what is to be done if for some reason the train is cancelled after the Block Indicator has been placed in the 'Train in Section' position, or has been put there by the signalman in error. How can it then be released? Welwyn Control provides such a release, requiring the signalman to turn a small wheel about 100 times whilst a disc revolves to tell him when he has done enough. The idea behind the monotonous turning of the wheel is that it gives the signalman time to reconsider whether he ought to be obtaining a release, or whether there might really be a train somewhere in the section. It guards against the dangers of misdirected impetuous action. It also gives the train time to arrive at the Home signal. It is an ingenious idea and it seems to have been effective. Long before 1935 several railway companies had devised similar systems but the releases could be obtained quickly and easily and several accidents resulted from over-hasty action by signalmen. The Midland Railway's Rotary Block was an example of this; it was a very safe system normally, but to obtain a release from 'Train in Section' all the signalman had to do was break a small piece of glass and press a button (similar to a fire-alarm). It was not something to be done lightly, because there was a lot of explaining to be done afterwards and reports to be written,

but it *could* be done hastily and without sufficient thought if the signalman was under pressure and anxious to avoid delay. Sykes Lock and Block system, widely used on several pre-Grouping companies, particularly those which formed the Southern Railway, and very highly regarded, had shortcomings of a similar nature.

So far as the signalman is concerned, the ultimate in safety must be the modern power signalbox, or Signalling Centre as it is sometimes called. It is a far cry from the early days of signalling when safety depended on the signalman faithfully carrying out his Rules and Regulations, with an accident being the likely result of any error. The science of signal engineering subsequently developed to provide a very high level of safety in manual signalboxes equipped with all the latest safety devices and controls, but it was still possible for signalmen to make potentially dangerous mistakes, or to operate the signals in such a way that the message they gave to drivers was less than completely unambiguous. Power signalboxes overcame those problems, although they were not designed primarily to improve safety levels, which were already very high, but rather to provide a more efficient means of planning and organising train movements in busy, complex or congested areas, an activity which goes under the title of train regulating. The power box signalman is now a train regulator, not employed to exercise his brawny muscles on pulling heavy

4 **5**

Above:
The work of dozens of old manual signalboxes is combined in one modern power signalbox. This is Carlisle. British Railways

Right:
A close-up of the station area on the Carlisle panel. The signalman appears to be about to cancel a route from platform 4 to the Up LNWR, shown by the white lights.
British Railways

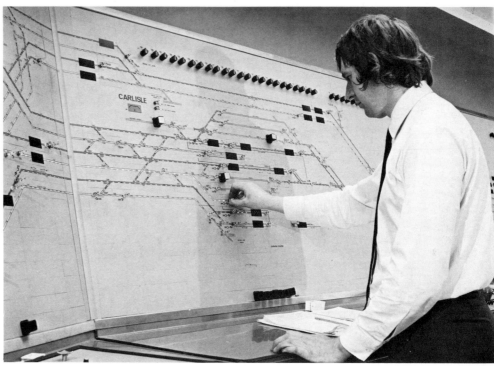

levers, with his brain power concentrated on the discipline and routine of the signalling Rules and Regulations, but rather to exercise his skill and judgement to achieve the best possible level of train regulation, optimising the use of the track, and keeping delays to a minimum. The job description has changed somewhat; the man description even more, and it is to the credit of so many signalmen that they have successfully adapted to the major change of environment, especially the change from being king of their own little castle to being members of a possibly quite large team in highly-technical surroundings, and not even seeing more than a fraction of the trains they deal with.

The most arresting features of the operating room in a modern power signalbox are the operating and indications panels. In some boxes they are combined, in others separate. The indications panel carries a diagrammatic representation of all the lines under the signalman's control. The signalman sets a route for a train by simply pressing two buttons — one at the start of the route and one at the end of it. If the route is available (ie if it has not already been promised to another train) the electrical equipment will do the rest. It will check if the route is available; if it is, it will move the points, lock them, guard them against other train movements and not clear the signals until all safety requirements have been satisfied. The signalman will know when this has happened (sometimes almost in a split second) because the route he has selected will light up, showing a row of white lights. He will know when the train comes along because red lights will appear along the route. He will know which train it is

Left:
Signalling in comfort in Watford Junction power signalbox. British Railways

Below:
The interior of King's Cross power signalbox, seen in this 1977 photograph, with the signalmen standing at their operating panels. Seated are the supervisor and his assistants, and the train announcer. British Rail (ER)

because its identification number will be displayed on the panel by the train describer equipment, and the signals, which will all be of the colour-light type, will revert to Danger behind it. The whole area will be track-circuited and very safe. There will be no bells (except emergency ones) and no block instruments.

It will probably have occurred to the reader by now that the process of setting routes and regulating trains is tailor-made for computerised operation, without the intervention of signalmen. This is already the normal practice on modern Metro systems with a fairly simple repetitive timetable, a limited network of lines and a high degree of punctuality. If sufficient capital is available it seems certain to be adopted on BR where similar conditions prevail, eg on large parts of the Southern Region and in

suburban areas around London and other major cities, in fact there are already several small-scale installations on the Southern Region, and a major system is planned for the new Yoker signalbox to deal with the north-Glasgow electrified service. It will be no less safe.

The verdict on the standard of safety in signalboxes must be that it is now very high indeed despite occasional lapses; but that is only half the story. Safety will only be assured if the message given by the signalman through the lineside signals is correctly received, interpreted, and acted upon by the driver; and that is the subject of the next chapter.

[1] See description on page 84.
[2] Studies had already been taking place following the collision near Whitehaven on 27 November 1973.

From the Driver's Cab

On 16 December 1971 at Lenton South Junction, Nottingham, there was a collision which not only aroused a great deal of interest among drivers, but also caused them some uneasiness. A heavy coal train, hauled by two Class 20 diesel-electric locomotives Nos 8115 and 8142, was proceeding slowly off the branch line on to the main Nottingham to Derby line at about 06.15 when it was run into head-on by the 01.30 parcels train from Liverpool to Nottingham, pulled by a Class 25 diesel-electric locomotive No 7605. The combined speed of the two trains at the moment of impact was something in the region of 40mph, and both drivers were killed by the force of the collision, together with the guard of the parcels train who was riding in the front cab of the locomotive.

The signalling in the area was of the modern multiple-aspect colour-light type, equipped with the Automatic Warning System, and was operated from Trent power signalbox, which had been opened only two years previously. According to the evidence of the guard of the coal train, and the signalman at Trent, the route had been set for the coal train to proceed from the branch line on to the Up main line to Trent and Derby, and the signal protecting the junction had been cleared to Green for it. The particular route along which the coal train had to traverse the junction required it to proceed for about 100yd in the 'facing' direction along the Down main line in order to reach a crossover which would take it on to the Up main line, and it was whilst travelling along the short section of Down main line that the collision occurred (the term 'facing direction' indicates a train movement in a direction opposite to the normal one for that section of line, eg an Up direction movement on a Down line). However, it should have been perfectly safe because the signals and signalling equipment (track circuits, interlocking, etc) were designed to cater for such movements.

The signalling equipment was exhaustively examined and tested after the accident, and no fault could be found which might have accounted for it. In the absence of any fault the main line signal protecting the movement off the branch would have been showing Red, with the signals in rear of it showing double Yellow and single Yellow respectively as they were approached by the driver of the parcels train. All three signals were provided with AWS and each one would have sounded a warning in the driving cab. If for any reason the driver had failed to react to those warnings and had not pressed his AWS acknowledgement button, the brakes would automatically have been applied. The train would then have been brought safely to a halt, at least from the double Yellow and single Yellow signals; and even from the Red signal the severity of the collision would have been reduced, as the distance from the AWS magnet serving the Red signal to the point of collision was 480yd, and the braking distance for the parcels train travelling at its maximum permitted speed of 45mph was only 500yd.

Lt-Col McNaughton held a Public Inquiry into this accident and concluded from the evidence that the driver of the parcels train had cancelled, in an automatic or subconscious manner, the AWS warnings he had received. No other conclusion was possible from the evidence, but drivers both in the Nottingham area and beyond found it difficult to comprehend how an experienced driver could have acted in such a manner. However, we now know from the driver's evidence at the Public Inquiry into the collision at Wembley on 11 October 1984 and from earlier accidents, that this can occur. One difficulty from a driver's point of view in such cases is that he cannot subsequently prove whether a signal was Green for him or not, even if he were to survive a crash (which is often not the case). If the evidence of the signalling equipment indicates that he has wrongly passed a signal at Danger he cannot prove otherwise, but neither can one prove absolutely that the signal was at Red when he passed it. The most that can be said is that no fault could afterwards be found in the signalling system, nor could anything be found to account for any failure. In effect the driver is left high and dry and some drivers would welcome a form of tachograph on the locomotive, to record both speed and adverse signals, and remove the element of doubt.

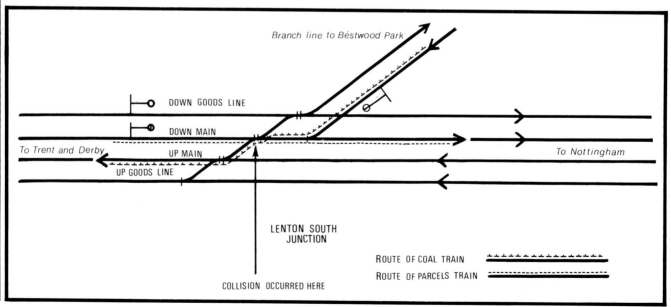

Below:
The destructive power of head-on collisions. Locomotives Nos 7605, 8115 and 8142 at Lenton South Junction near Nottingham after the accident on 16 December 1971.
Jack Hooke

Left:
The rear cab of Class 25 locomotive No 7605 was completely destroyed by the vehicles of its own parcels train. Jack Hooks

Bottom:
A Class 150/1 Sprinter unit, heading towards Nottingham, passes over the precise spot of the 1971 crash at Lenton South Junction. This is the view in 1986 looking westwards towards Trent and Derby. Author

The driver is similarly exposed where speed checks are concerned. These are carried out regularly using a variety of methods, including radar speed meters. The preferred system is the 'measured track circuit', the length of which is known. The speed is calculated by taking the amount of time which elapses between the initial occupation of that particular track circuit and the initial occupation of the next one. The procedure can be carried out manually but it is preferable, and easier in modern power signalboxes, for it to be done automatically by the signalling equipment, with the results being printed out. If a train is then noticed to have been exceeding its maximum allowed speed the driver is seen and challenged. In the case of manual speed checks there is always a possibility of observer error, but with an automatic system there is practically none.

To return to the Lenton South Junction accident, the possibility was explored as to whether it would have been possible for the signalman to have changed his mind and altered the route which he had set, thus creating a potentially dangerous situation. The supposition is as follows:

No 37107 takes its train through the crossover at Haughley Junction after coming off the Cambridge line with the 12.55 Peterborough-Parkeston Quay, a few weeks after the collision between two mail trains, whose wreckage is still sheeted-up on site. John C. Baker

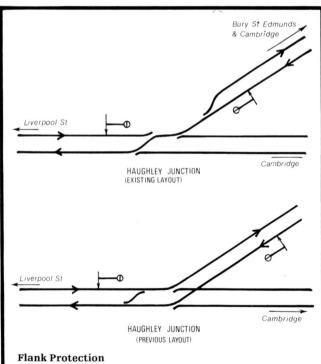

Flank Protection

With the existing layout, if a train from Liverpool Street wrongly runs past the junction signal at Danger it can collide head-on with a train coming on to the main line from the Cambridge direction. This could not have happened on the previous layout because the train from Liverpool Street would have been diverted on to the Branch towards Cambridge out of harm's way; the interlocking of the junction points would have ensured this.

'If the signalman had decided to run the parcels train over the junction first, and had cleared all his signals for it, and had then changed his mind and decided to let the coal train go first, he could have put his signals to Danger against the parcels train just as it was approaching the junction and too late for it to stop in time, and cleared his signals for the coal train. The coal train would then have moved off on to the junction to be met head-on by the approaching parcels train whose driver had been unable to stop.'

It sounds possible although most unlikely, but in fact the signalling equipment has been designed to make it not only unlikely but impossible. This is achieved by a process known as approach-locking. Once the signalman has set a route for a train, that route cannot be cancelled and a conflicting route set, until the train has passed over it or until a release mechanism has timed itself out. This release generally takes two minutes, sometimes more, and is designed to ensure that there is sufficient time, after the junction signal has been put back to Danger, for a train to come safely to a halt at it before the points can be moved, or alternatively if it is too close to the signal to be able to stop there it will have time to pass safely through the junction before another route can be set. At some locations approach-locking becomes operative as soon as the junction signal is cleared from Red; at others, where circumstances might require re-routeing to be done fairly frequenttly, approach-locking does not become operative until the junction signal has been cleared from Red *and* an approaching train has reached the sighting point of the furthest signal approaching the junction which would change from Green to Caution in the event of the junction signal being replaced to Danger.

We have noticed before how new technologies create new hazards. It is a paradox that despite the signalling in the Nottingham area as a whole being safer after the opening of Trent power signalbox than before, this accident might not have happened with the old signalling because of what is known as 'flank protection'. With a traditionally-signalled junction the trailing points leading from the branch line cannot be moved to allow a train to travel from the branch on to the main line until the parallel facing points have been set *towards* the branch. This ensures that if a train approaching the junction in the facing direction accidentally runs past the junction signal at Danger it will be diverted on to the branch out of harm's way instead of crashing headlong into a train coming off the branch. There was an accident, similar in some respects to the one at Lenton South Junction, which occurred on 22 June 1982 at Haughley Junction where the former Great Eastern main line from Liverpool Street goes forward to Norwich and a line to Cambridge via Bury St Edmunds turns off. The former double junction had been re-modelled by the Civil Engineer to reduce costs and simplify maintenance, but it also had the effect of removing flank protection. At 01.18 the 01.01 mail train from Ipswich to Peterborough accidentally overran the junction signal which was at Danger and collided with its opposite number, the 23.10 mail from Peterborough to Ipswich, which was just coming off the Cambridge branch on to the main line under Clear signals. Four members of the two train crews and two Post Office staff were injured and taken to hospital, but fortunately no one was killed.

Modern signalling controls should make such simplified layouts perfectly safe, but to be absolutely sure there must be 100% certainty of obedience to signals by drivers. It is not without significance that AWS was provided at both Lenton South Junction and Haughley Junction, and at both it was ineffective. At the former it is assumed that the driver cancelled the AWS warning subconsciously without

Left:
Switch diamonds in the Up main/Down Grimsby line at Werrington Junction, a few miles north of Peterborough. This photograph was taken about 30 years ago after the junction had been remodelled to allow high speeds to and from the branch. Ian Allan Library

Above:
A close-up of switch diamonds at Gretna Junction, looking north. The route is set for a train from the Dumfries direction. The complicated locking and detection apparatus can clearly be seen. This photograph was taken before the junction was remodelled under the Carlisle resignalling scheme.
British Railways

reacting to it; at the latter the train crew mismanaged the braking to such an extent that not only were they unable to stop at the junction signal but carried on for a further 230yd before hitting the other mail train. The benefit to the Civil Engineer of such simplified layouts is the elimination of the diamond-shaped crossing where the two tracks cross each other, saving both capital outlay and maintenance costs. It also eliminates a possible source of derailment if the crossing is not maintained to a sufficiently high standard. The debit to the Operator is the inability to run trains on to and off the branch simultaneously, and the creation of an additional potential hazard; on the other hand, it may allow higher speeds through the junction.

Signalling equipment is designed to 'fail safe'. A failure will have the effect of either replacing a Clear signal to Danger, or preventing a Danger signal from being cleared. This is known as a 'right-side' failure and is not at all uncommon given the tens of thousands of signals, points and track circuits on Britain's railways. On the other hand it can be very disconcerting to a driver who has passed a Green signal, suddenly to find himself confronted with a Red. He has no means of knowing immediately whether it has been caused by an equipment fault or whether the signal has been put to Red in an emergency; and he may easily have a few anxious moments if he passes the signal

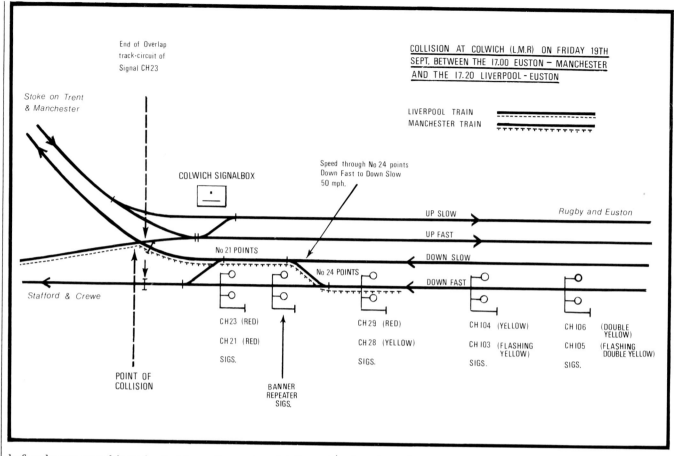

COLLISION AT COLWICH (L.M.R) ON FRIDAY 19TH
SEPT. BETWEEN THE 17.00 EUSTON – MANCHESTER
AND THE 17.20 LIVERPOOL - EUSTON

before he can stop his train. To him, a Green signal followed by a Red is irregular and a wrong-side failure, but in fact it is very unlikely to be so; the signalling system is carrying out its designed function of failing-safe, ie a right-side failure. It is sometimes difficult to convince drivers that it is so, especially if failures occur frequently in particular areas due perhaps to equipment which is nearing the end of its life, or where high standards of equipment reliability may be difficult to achieve for technical or other reasons, such as unsatisfactory ground conditions affecting the operation of track circuits.

Signalling equipment nowadays is extremely complex, and the finer points of design and operation may be outside the knowledge and experience of many drivers. It is fortunate, and safe, that drivers customarily obey implicitly and with complete confidence the message given by signals without pondering too deeply on the reasons why a signal may be giving a particular message, or changing its message. Accidents caused by wrong-side failures are extremely rare, although one occurred at Bushbury Junction on the line from Stafford to Birmingham on 13 August 1979 when the 13.29 express from Manchester to Birmingham was derailed at about 35mph. No passengers were hurt but the driver was badly injured. Part of the junction layout known as a 'switch diamond' was not properly closed and this should have locked the junction signal at Danger, but it did not do so. A bearing screw in the point-operating machine had become disengaged and allowed the equipment which detects the position of the switch diamond to register that they were properly closed, when in fact they were standing slightly open. The irregular detection allowed the junction signal to be cleared from Red, and the train was derailed as it passed through the slightly-open switch diamond. The very rare wrong-side failures which occur are sometimes caused by irregular point detection incorrectly allowing a signal to show Clear when it ought to be held at Red. It is almost unknown for a wrong-side failure to allow a signal to show Clear and lead a train into the danger of collision with another train.

It may seem at first sight that the messages given by railway signals are essentially simple. Red means stop; Green means go, and Yellow or Double Yellow means slow down because you are approaching a Red. In semaphore signalling a Distant signal (which is a yellow arm) in the horizontal position means 'Caution, the Home signal is at Danger'. If the arm is raised or lowered 45° it means 'Clear, and all the Stop signals worked from the same signalbox are also Clear'. A Stop signal has a red arm, and may be called the Home signal or the Starting signal (or the Outer Home signal, or the Advanced Starting signal). When the arm is horizontal it means 'Danger, Stop'. When the arm is raised or lowered 45° it means 'Proceed'. Every schoolboy knows that, or ought to. But things are not quite so simple, as we have already seen in Chapter 2 when we discussed the working of the signals at Longforgan signalbox, and some of it may not be evident to drivers, or even known by them. Let us consider a few examples in the field of multiple-aspect colour-light signalling.

There is a safety margin known as an overlap, usually 200yd long, beyond most signals that can show a Red aspect, and it affects the working of signals in the following way. A signal (call it signal A) will not clear from Red until the previous train to pass it has proceeded through the signal section beyond, has passed clear of the next signal (B) and has passed completely clear of the overlap track circuit beyond Signal B. Where speeds are low the length of the overlap may be reduced, and in some station areas where speeds are very low, say 10 to 15mph, there may be no overlaps at all. Overlaps are an important part of the safety of junction working; after a route has been set up to a signal at a junction, the overlap of that signal is assumed to be part of the route; in other words it has been 'promised' to that train and cannot at the same time be promised to another train approaching from a different direction. In many cases, signals at a junction are located at overlap distance from the fouling point (ie the place where trains may cross each other's route or collide with each other) and this allows trains to approach close to the junction to wait their turn whilst other trains are using it. The concept of a safety overlap comes from the early days of Block Signalling, and for semaphore signals it is 440yd. Its purpose now is really to allow for the possibility of the driver mismanaging his brake and accidentally running past a Danger signal; it does not provide much of a safeguard against a driver who has failed to see the Distant signal and has only just applied his brakes when close to the signal at Danger, nor is it intended to act as a safeguard in such circumstances.

The majority of cases where drivers accidentally overrun a signal at Danger result from mismanagement of the brake, or from anticipating that the signal will clear when it does not; and not from the driver missing a signal altogether or misunderstanding its message. Usually the train stops with the locomotive only a few yards beyond the signal, and the driver reports to the signalman by means of the telephone at the signal (nearly all colour-light signals have a telephone) that he has 'just slipped by an engine-length'. The signalman will probably already know because he may have seen the overlap track circuit become illuminated on his indication panel. Drivers may not know how long (or short) an overlap track circuit is, but they can sometimes tell by the insulated rail joint at the end of it. They are unlikely to know in a station area but will be used to seeing fouling movements taking place a short distance ahead of them which they would not see out on the main line. At some stations such as Birmingham New Street, a restricted

approach arrangement is in operation, whereby the signal controlling entry to the station will not clear from Red if the platform Starting signal is a Red, until the train is very close to it.

At junctions where drivers have to reduce speed in order to turn off the main line safely, or for example where they cross from a Fast line to a Slow line, the junction signal may be held at Red even though the route beyond it may have been set, until the train is assumed (through track circuit occupation) to have reduced its speed to a safe level. This process is known as 'approach control' and is very, very common. At high-speed junctions flashing-yellow aspects may be used to give the driver plenty of warning and avoid his having to reduce speed unduly. Drivers are accustomed to approach-control without necessarily knowing how it is achieved technically.

Drivers are vulnerable in their driving cabs if an accident occurs, and several of them are killed or seriously injured every year as we have already seen. However, if a driver causes an accident and survives, he may be charged with manslaughter if fatalities occur, or with endangering life if no one is killed. Such prosecutions have followed a number of the accidents mentioned in this book but have rarely been successful. For the prosecution to succeed, a high degree of negligence or recklessness has to be proved, and juries have been very reluctant to convict. Perhaps both they and the judge feel that the driver has already suffered

Below:
A view of Colwich Junction looking north after being relaid following the collision between two expresses on 19 September 1986, showing the Crewe line to the left and the Manchester via Stoke line to the right. The impact took place on the diamond crossing (top centre). Author

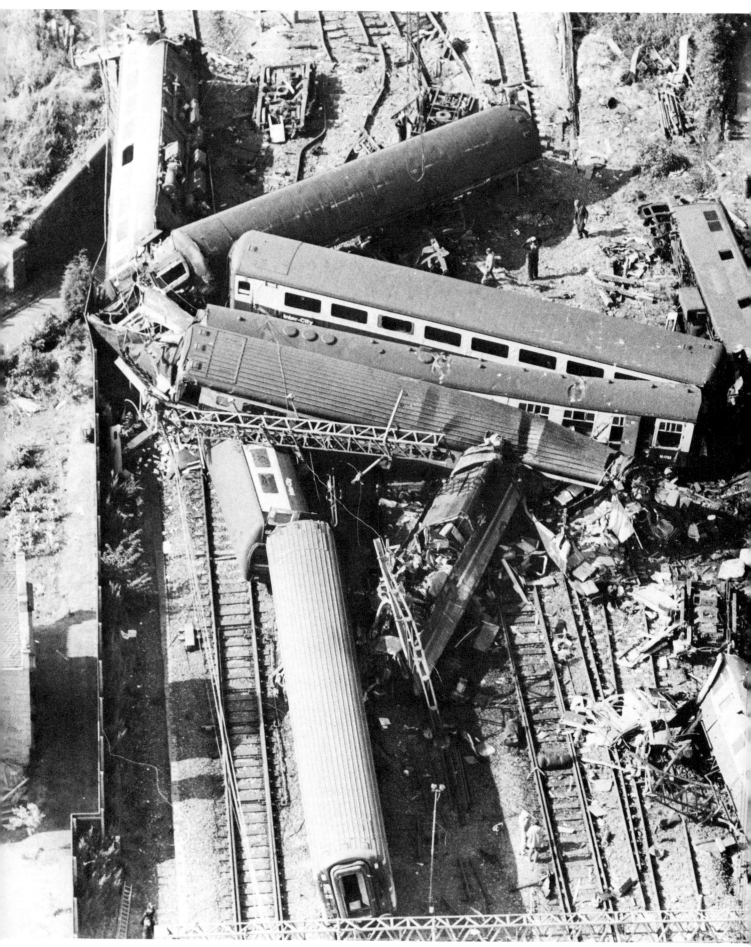

enough, with death and destruction on his conscience for the rest of his life as a result of some understandable human failing, without having to undergo further punishment and disgrace. It is interesting to note that these matters had come to prominence as long ago as 1840, when Section 13 of the Railway Regulation Act provided penalties for railway servants guilty of misconduct or neglect, or who were drunk when on duty. These powers are still in force today, although contained in later Acts. The most recent prosecutions followed the accidents at Nuneaton in June 1975 and Morpeth in June 1984. In the earlier case the driver was indicted on six counts of manslaughter but was acquitted by the jury on all charges. In the latter case the driver was found 'not guilty' by the jury of endangering the lives of 71 passengers through wilful omission or negligence. It ought perhaps to be pointed out here that the conclusions of an Inspecting Officer of the Department of Transport following a Public Inquiry into an accident are his personal conclusions based on the weight of evidence. His task is to establish the cause of an accident and he is not concerned with criminal negligence, nor with civil liability. He will always reach a conclusion, which may be firm or less so depending on the nature of the evidence. It is sometimes not possible to be 100% sure, especially if the driver is killed and his cab is wrecked, thus destroying a lot of the evidence. Evidence may allow a particular conclusion to be drawn, but it may not be sufficiently strong to result in a successful prosecution, or a successful charge under the railway's own internal disciplinary scheme. It might also be added that every serious accident is formally investigated by a team of railway experts before any Public Inquiry is held, and the team are required to reach a conclusion, based on the evidence, as to the probable cause. They are not required to make recommendations as to remedial measures — that is done separately by accident experts — unlike the Department of Transport Inspecting Officers, who do both. The railway's own accident reports are not published although copies are made available to the Inspecting Officers, whose reports *are* published.

A driver's job, in essence, is to run his train to time, to brake safely, and to obey all signals and speed limits, and to do this he needs to be thoroughly acquainted with the routes over which he works. Every six months he will 'sign' for such routes. Once a driver has passed his initial rigorous examination it is left almost entirely to his own sense of responsibility to keep himself fully acquainted with the Rules, and up to date. He will not be examined again, and the most he will have to do is to produce his Rule Book annually for inspection and satisfy an Inspector who will ride with him once a year for a few hours that he is still driving properly. The Inspector may ask questions about driving techniques, but not about the Rules. That is taboo; the Unions will not agree to it. These arrangements are not entirely satisfactory and it would be more effective if drivers were given periodic refresher courses not only to keep their knowledge up to date but also to ensure that they were aware of changes and understood them.

It is interesting to note that following two recent accidents in France caused by drivers failing to observe temporary speed restrictions, the French National Rail-

Left:
Locomotives and coaches lie scattered in all directions after the high-speed head-on crash at Colwich Junction on 19 September 1986. Looking at the mass of tangled wreckage, it is hard to believe that not a single passenger was killed, even through both trains were full. In the centre can be seen No 86429 *The Times*, which had been at the head of the Liverpool-Euston train, whilst to the right of the tracks is the locomotive of the Euston-Manchester service, No 86211 *City of Milton Keynes*. Times Newspapers Ltd

ways (SNCF) ordered oral Rule examinations for all staff responsible for safety. Drivers, who are examined on their route knowledge and safety procedures every three months, came out on strike. The proposal was dropped.

As we have seen from the accidents discussed and reviewed so far, no good case can be made out for having an additional man in the driving cab to help the driver, at least at speeds up to 100mph. When maximum speeds rose from 100mph to 125mph it was in some ways a leap into the unknown, and there was no sure way of knowing how drivers would react to the stress of signals coming at them 25% faster, but in fact modern signalling is so good, and so easy for drivers to understand, that there seems to be no case for an extra driver solely from the point of view of obedience to signals. Multiple-aspect colour-light signalling with AWS has considerably improved the driver's lot and removed much of the stress. There are, however, other factors, and these will now be discussed.

It is necessary to have a firm policy regarding the technical aids to be provided in the driving cab to guard against the effects of inattention, sleepiness or incapacity of the driver. AWS is provided to guard against all three but may be over-ridden involuntarily. The driver's safety device (the 'deadman's pedal') has been shown in this book to have been ineffective on several critical occasions, and modifications have been carried out to improve its efficiency. A centrally-pivoted design was introduced which required the driver to maintain it in a centrally-balanced position, and later a vigilance device was introduced which caused a bleeper to sound every minute and required the driver to release and reset the DSD. Whilst fairly effective, it was found to be cumbersome and intrusive, and modifications were planned which had the effect of postponing the bleep for a minute every time the driver proved that he was alert by operating any of the controls, such as brake, horn, power controller, etc. A great deal of thought, research and experimentation have gone into this subject, not only on BR but also abroad. It is a worldwide problem, but so far as BR is concerned it is clear that in order to increase safety something better is needed which concentrates *directly* on ensuring that the brake is applied at the right time rather than *indirectly* on ensuring that the driver stays alert. The latter does not in itself automatically guarantee that the brake will be applied when required.

There appear to be three alternatives:

1 An automatic system, whereby any necessity to brake, either for adverse signals, or for speed restrictions, is taken out of the driver's hands and done for him automatically. Metro systems nowadays often employ this method of working but it may be unsuitable for main-line working on two counts — expense, and the effect on the driver of having too little to do.

2 A monitoring system, which continuously checks the train's speed but only interposes when it detects that the train is going too fast. The speed and braking of the train would be left entirely in the driver's hands provided that he handled his train correctly. If he failed to do so for any reason the back-up system would over-ride him and take charge. By this means the dangers of drowsiness, inattention, incapacity or errors of judgement would be guarded against. Vigilance devices would not be needed, at least for safety; at the worst a train might pass through a station where it is booked to stop, without doing so, but it could not do so at an unsafe speed.

3 An advisory system such as the present BR standard AWS which has served the cause of safety well over the years, but which is now showing its age. The driver is expected to keep sufficiently alert at all times in order to use the advice he receives from the system, but in

practical human terms it requires a standard of performance which is not consistently achievable across the length and breadth of the country all day and every day, and vigilance devices have had to be developed to fill the gap. They do so reasonably well but are a cumbersome addition; if the driver is running past a series of Caution signals and speed restrictions his AWS horn will sound at every one, and the warning it gives has to be acknowledged and acted upon. On top of that his vigilance device will bleep every minute, requiring him to re-set his DSD pedal. Furthermore the horn and bleep may coincide. Altogether it is an untidy arrangement and hardly appropriate for high-speed running.

What BR needs to do now if it wishes to enhance its already high safety standards and avoid more 'Wembleys' is to advance from an advisory system to a monitoring system, one that recognises when a driver ought to be braking for a Red signal or a speed restriction, and automatically applies the brake without the possibility of being over-ridden if the train is going too fast. A highly sophisticated and expensive automatic system is not necessary, nor is cab signalling. Even at 125mph the driver is perfectly capable of observing, interpreting and reacting to signals in plenty of time, and probably would be at speeds of up to 140mph. The basic requirement of a monitoring system is that it should continuously detect the state of the signals ahead, by interrogating equipment laid in the 'four-foot' (the space between the two rails), so that when the train came within braking distance of a Red signal or speed restriction the appropriate speed calculated from the braking curve could be displayed on the driver's instrument panel. If the driver did not keep his speed below the level indicated, the brakes would automatically be applied. For the purpose of calculating braking distance, the track-borne equipment would indicate distance and gradient; the train-borne equipment would monitor the speed. A train-borne computer, programmed with details of the train's braking capability, would continuously calculate the braking curve and display the required safe speed to the driver. It would also monitor the train's actual speed and interpose if it exceeded the safe speed. The track-borne equipment would also provide details of the maximum line speed, together with any speed restrictions, and the train-borne equipment would calculate the associated braking curve. There would be no need for the driver to acknowledge a warning at a Caution signal; for it would be the degree of the driver's reaction to the approaching Red that would determine whether the automatic safety back-up intervened. In normal circumstances the safety back-up would *not* intervene; it would merely watch and guard. The driver would drive and brake his train in an entirely normal manner. He would have no need to look at the 'Safe-speed' indicator, because it goes without saying that if he drove his train correctly he would never travel at more than the safe speed. The danger of subconscious cancellation of an AWS warning would disappear. The driver would still look ahead, and observe and react to signals exactly as now. He would not need an AWS warning at a Caution signal, merely a location reminder for him to observe the signal. Inattention or drowsiness approaching a Red signal would always result in the brakes being applied, because there would be no override button which could be operated subconsciously. This system would leave the driver firmly in control, an important feature to avoid the 'zombie' effect of taking too much control and initiative out of the driver's hands. Double-manning of the driving cab would be unnecessary at any speed.

One of the disadvantages inherent in such a monitoring system is that the braking curve has to be calculated on the

Above:
A railway breakdown crane prepares to lift an overturned BR Mk 3 coach into the fields behind following the Colwich disaster. Gary S. Smith

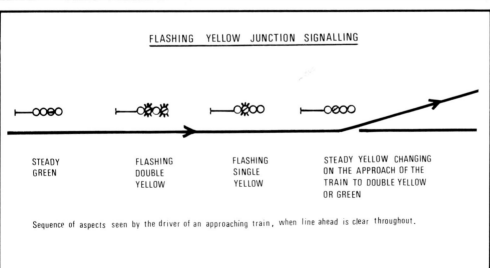

FLASHING YELLOW JUNCTION SIGNALLING

| STEADY GREEN | FLASHING DOUBLE YELLOW | FLASHING SINGLE YELLOW | STEADY YELLOW CHANGING ON THE APPROACH OF THE TRAIN TO DOUBLE YELLOW OR GREEN |

Sequence of aspects seen by the driver of an approaching train, when line ahead is clear throughout.

basis of 'worst performance', that is to say it must be based on a poor brake, a wet or greasy rail, heavy loads, etc. The resulting calculated braking curve will therefore be too restrictive in almost every case. The driver, on the other hand, takes all these factors into account in deciding how to operate the brake and cannot only be infinitely variable in deciding where to commence braking but can also adjust his level of braking throughout the duration of the operation if he wishes to give different weight to any particular factor. The machine cannot reproduce this human flexibility but it would be too restrictive to accept a 'worst performance' braking curve all the time. What is proposed, therefore, is that the system should incorporate a brake performance selector, which the driver would pre-set according to his judgement of conditions, ranging from worst performance at one extreme to best performance at the other. This would then allow the system to calculate the braking curve to correspond as closely as possible with the way in which the driver actually brakes, and so avoid an over-restrictive indication of the required speed, or premature intervention of the automatic braking.

What are the advantages of such a system?

1 It leaves the driving of the train in the driver's hands. Does not impair his skill, or his pride in his job. Avoids the zombie effect.
2 It provides an infallible safety back-up. No more 'Wembleys' or 'Morpeths'.
3 Double-manning is unnecessary.
4 The driver will continue to look ahead for signals and warning signs. It is important that he should not spend time looking at his control panel or try to do both.
5 It incorporates both signals and speed restrictions/limits in one system.
6 It avoids the need for the driver to press the AWS acknowledgement button at Caution or Red signals.
7 When a driver is braking for a Red signal which is out of sight he will know immediately if it clears, because the advisory speed indicated will rise. He will then be able to accelerate sooner than he can at present.
8 Approach control of signals at junctions would no longer be necessary. The junction signal for the low-speed route could be cleared to Green as soon as the points were set (provided the line ahead was clear). The track-borne apparatus approaching the junction would announce which way the junction was set and the appropriate speed restriction. This information would be received by the locomotive computer, which would calculate the braking curve required. The computer would also tell the driver of the speed required at the junction, leaving him to brake to that speed but monitoring that he was doing so.

In case this proposal should be thought to be too revolutionary, it might be mentioned that the French and Italian Railways have had something similar for 20 years or more. Even BR were experimenting with the idea, but it was killed by the lack of a settled and established political, organisational and economic framework. Long-term development and research and the long-term investment required, indeed faith in the long-term future, are all needed for a project of this nature but are very difficult to achieve in all the many upheavals, both internal and external, that have plagued BR in the last 30 years. There is little doubt that if during those 30 years BR had enjoyed the same happy, progressive and supportive relationship with, and generous treatment from, its political masters as its continental railway colleagues have had from theirs, we too would have a more effective train protection system by now. But even if work were to start at once it would be the turn of the century before real benefits began to be felt, given 5-10 years for development, design and proving, and a further five to 10 years for installation on high-speed routes. There is no time to be lost.

If proof were needed that the present AWS is inadequate, it was provided in full measure at Colwich on the West Coast main line of the London Midland Region between Lichfield and Stafford on the evening of Friday 19 September 1986. At Colwich, proceeding northwards, the line divides, the main line continuing towards Stafford and Crewe, with the line to Stoke-on-Trent and Manchester turning off towards the right. Nearly 900 passengers had a miraculous escape from death when a Down Manchester express wrongly passed a signal at Danger and stopped with its electric locomotive plumb in the path of an Up express from Liverpool to Euston closely approaching at about 100mph under Clear signals.

This accident, which astonishingly resulted in only one death, that of the unfortunate and innocent driver of the express from Liverpool, was a classic case, and neatly encapsulates five of the perennial hazards which we have discussed so far: Inadequate AWS (as at Wembley 1984); lack of flank protection (as at Lenton South Junction 1971); the perils of change; jumping to conclusions (as at Nuneaton 1975); adequacy, or otherwise, of refresher training for drivers.

The railway at Colwich is electrified at 25kV ac. Modern multiple-aspect colour-light signalling is provided, and

AWS is installed at every signal. The signalling system in force is the Track Circuit Block system. Shortly before the accident a relatively new system of junction signalling had been installed in the route of the Manchester express, which incorporated Flashing-Yellow signals to give the driver a positive advance indication that the facing points ahead were set for a diverging route over which speed must be reduced (see sketch of this arrangement). Prior to its introduction, a safe speed at the diverging junction had been achieved by the normal procedure of maintaining the junction signal at Danger for the lower speed route until the train was close to it, thus causing the speed of the train to be reduced. However, at junctions laid out to permit higher speeds of up to 70mph or more on the diverging route the normal procedure, known as approach control, was found to be too restrictive and caused the speed of an approaching train to be reduced unnecessarily early and sometimes too severely, therefore the 'Flashing-Yellow' system was devised to allow trains to travel through diverging junctions at the designed speed without any unnecessary loss of time. The first example was installed at Didcot in March 1979, since when they have become increasingly widespread and common.

On the evening of the accident the signalman at Colwich observed from his illuminated panel that both expresses were approaching at more or less the same time and he decided to give priority to the Liverpool-Euston train, as he was fully entitled to do. This meant that the Manchester train would have to wait its turn over the junction and might have to stop at signal CH 23 protecting the junction. The Manchester train was approaching on the Down Fast line (see drawing) and the signalman had set No 24 points to divert the train to the Down Slow line to bring it up to No 23 signal. This caused the following sequence of signals to be presented to the Manchester driver:

CH 105 Flashing Double-Yellow (Advance indication of diverging route ahead of next signal but one)
CH 103 One Flashing-Yellow. (Preliminary Caution and indication of diverging route ahead of next signal)
CH 28 Steady Single Yellow, with route indicator. (Route ahead set for a diverging direction. Next signal at Danger)
Banner Repeater for CH 23 Erected because a new road bridge had obscured the driver's approach view of signal CH 23. Its function is to give the driver an advance indication of the aspect shown at signal CH 23. It showed Danger, but as it is merely a Repeater signal the Driver was not required to stop at it.
CH 23 Red (Danger-Stop)

According to the driver's evidence at the Department of Transport Public Inquiry at Crewe on 23 October 1986, held by Maj Olver, he saw the signal aspects exactly as described and braked from 100mph to about 80mph at the Flashing Double-Yellow, then to 60mph at the Flashing Single Yellow, reducing speed further to 45mph at the crossover from Down Fast to Down Slow. Here he made the fatal error. He said that he was surprised to see signal CH 23 at Red and expected it to clear; then when he could see it wasn't going to clear he made an emergency brake application. At this awful moment he saw the Liverpool-Euston express approaching at full speed on a collision course. He still hoped that he would be able to stop in time, but when he realised a collision was inevitable he jumped clear at the last moment. His train had almost stopped. 'I thought I was going to be killed', he said.

What was the nature of the driver's error? He thought that Flashing Yellows meant that the line ahead was clear through the junction to the Stoke line past signal No 23, hence his bewilderment when that signal was at Red. He then assumed that the signal must be Approach-Controlled and would clear as he approached. His fundamental error was almost one of nomenclature. He did not regard the Down Fast to Down Slow route at No 24 points as a junction, whereas the signalling system did. It was as simple as that. Having interpreted the signalling aspects that he received to mean that he had the road right through to the Stoke line, his mind became programmed to that effect. When he realised that something was wrong it was just a few seconds too late to recover the situation and save the day.

So what of our five principles?

Inadequate AWS. The BR system warned the driver that CH 23 signal was not Clear, but he already knew that. Its failure was that it did not enforce its warning, indeed it was not designed to do so in such circumstances. The improved system proposed earlier in this chapter would have ensured that the train stopped at CH 23 signal despite anything the driver did, or any mistake or misunderstanding on his part. It does not require Flashing Yellows or approach control.

Lack of flank protection. In a conventional layout the driver of the Manchester train would have been diverted out of harm's way. At Colwich he only had a bare 200yd overrun margin. Without an AWS which *guarantees* that a train will stop at a Danger signal, such lack of flank protection can be deadly.

The perils of change. The flashing yellows had only just been introduced at Colwich and the driver misunderstood them.

Jumping to conclusions. When the driver saw signal CH 23 at Red he was surprised, but thought that it must be at Red because it was approach-controlled and would clear as he got near to it. In reality it was at Red because another train was going to cross that line 200yds head.

Adequacy or otherwise of refresher training for drivers. This speaks for itself. The system should have ensured that the driver knew.

But in the ultimate reckoning, whatever we may say about the cause of the accident, and who did what and why, the railway organisation should have ensured either that the mistake didn't take place, or that there was an infallible safety back-up if it did. It did neither.

Left:
Between the mangled remains of the two locomotives at Colwich lie the heaped-up bodies of three generations of coaching stock. Gary S. Smith

# Single Line Operations

A number of times in recent years we have opened our newspapers to be greeted by photographs of the horrifying devastation caused by that most destructive of all railway accidents — the collision at high speed of two trains running head-on into each other on a single line. Fortunately, at least for railway passengers in Britain, these collisions have happened abroad but in countries that would normally regard their railway systems as being at least as technically advanced as ours — France, Germany, Holland and Canada.

Britain's railways were mainly constructed with double track, except for short branches, and lines in sparsely-populated areas. Yet despite many closures there are still hundreds of miles of single track in use today. The standard of safety on Britain's single lines has been very high for many years, thanks to a simple but ingenious piece of equipment known as the 'token'. Each section of single line between two signalboxes has its own token which every train through the section must carry, and as there is only one token available at any one time it follows that safety is assured, for not only are head-on collisions prevented but the possibility of a train crashing into one in front going in the same direction is also avoided. The token is sometimes very simple — just a piece of wood looking like 12 or 18in of broom handle, bearing a plate with the name of the section on it. In other cases, where it is part of the signalling equipment, it may be made of metal and shaped rather like a key (known appropriately as a key-token) or it may be a thick plastic disc rather like a large chocolate biscuit.

The system requires, of course, that drivers do not enter a section without a token (and that they obey the signals). They are strictly enjoined not to enter a section without a token. Very strictly indeed. The General Appendix goes so far as to utter almost blood-curdling threats: 'A driver will render himself liable to dismissal if he leaves . . . without the token'. Nowhere else in the whole panoply of Rules and Regulations is discipline enforced in such a forthright manner. Only in a general sense is dismissal mentioned elsewhere in the Rules. The offence of entering a single line section without a token has always been regarded as one of the most serious it is possible for a driver to commit — the Rule Book of a century ago contained the same wording, thus illustrating the remarkable durability of railway Rules whilst the rest of the world is changing out of all recognition around them.

A moment's thought, however, will reveal that the practice of having only one token for a section has its limitations. It requires trains to proceed from opposite ends of the section alternately (unless some means are adopted of conveying the token to the other end). It demands a rigid timetable and good punctuality. Special trains can only be operated with difficulty. These are problems which plagued the Central Wales line when it was worked on this system.

Necessity being the mother of invention, a way was found round the difficulty by having a number of tokens locked in a machine at each end of the section, the machines being electrically interlinked so that only one token for the section can be taken 'out' at any one time. This arrangement is known as the Electric Token Block system and has been the mainstay of single line working for over a century, resulting in a very high standard of safety apart from rare lapses. We have already met the Regulation of Railways Act of 1889 in connection with Block Systems. That Act also gave the Board of Trade powers to order that single lines should be worked on one of three systems, which included the Single Token and the Electric Token Block system.

For many years the two systems mentioned served their purpose adequately and efficiently but eventually it came to be recognised that the Electric Token system was in some cases rather elaborate and restrictive. What was really needed was a simpler but still safe system that did away with the token, and allowed trains to pass signalboxes without having to slow down to exchange the tokens. Another requirement was the ability to close signalboxes for a few hours without the problems this caused with electric token working. So far as trains following each other in the same direction over the single line were concerned, the same arrangements as applied on double lines ought to suffice — no token being necessary. The crux of the matter was to ensure that a train could not be admitted into a section if there was already one passing through it in either direction. Thus was the aptly named 'Tokenless Block System' born. It operates as follows. Track circuits are provided at each end of the section and after a train has occupied and cleared the track circuits on its entry into the section the Starting signal at neither end of the section can again be cleared (they are electrically locked) for another train in either direction until the first train has occupied and cleared track circuits at the far end of the section. Safety is assured provided drivers obey the signals, and the fundamental basis of signalling is that drivers do obey signals, although caution compels an admission that occasionally they do not. One of Canada's worst railway accidents occurred on Saturday 8 February 1986 on the Canadian National Railway in Alberta when a 114-car freight train wrongly left a section of double track and moved on to a single line to collide head-on at speed with an approaching transcontinental passenger train, killing 23 people and injuring 60. There was no token system in use and the accident would almost certainly not have happened if there had been. The Electric Token system may be old-fashioned but it is very safe.

A refinement of Tokenless Block operates in areas worked from power signalboxes where sections of single lines (usually short ones) are track-circuited throughout. After a signal has been cleared for a train to enter a section no signal can be cleared for a second train to enter the section from either end until all the track circuits have cleared after the passage of the first train. It is known as Track Circuit Block and also operates on those sections of double line where trains may pass in either direction on one track. It is very common over short stretches of line in junction areas (eg Lenton South Junction, see Chapter 8). A more recent development has been the signalling of long stretches of double line in such a manner that each track can be used by trains in either direction. The practice is known as 'bi-directional working' and allows one track to be handed over at quiet times to the Civil Engineer for maintenance. It is in use between Didcot, Swindon and beyond, and on parts of the Brighton line, and is being installed on the Midland main line south of Leicester. Without such a system, when one track has to be handed over for maintenance, trains in both directions have to be worked over the remaining line by a cumbersome, complicated and time-consuming procedure known in railway parlance as 'single-line working', often resulting in such serious delays to trains that operators divert trains over longer routes to avoid the affected section. Bi-directional signalling is expensive and in order to make the fullest use of it, facing crossovers capable of being used at fairly high speed need to be provided at regular intervals, thus increasing the cost. When a major resignalling scheme is being developed, any bi-directional proposals are always subjected to very close scrutiny on grounds of cost, and financial pressures being what they are, such proposals are often pruned or omitted altogether, which is a great pity because the cost is only marginal in relation to the scheme as a whole, and in consequence the remainder of the scheme (the main part) is not being used as productively as it might be, nor to its full potential. Furthermore it is much more expensive to go back afterwards and attempt to superimpose the bi-directional element on an already completed scheme. The Rugby-Coventry-Birmingham line is a good example of this; the bi-directional facility is badly needed there but no one has yet been able to make a sufficiently compelling financial case.

It might be mentioned in passing that the use of track circuits to prove that a section of single line is clear has a longer history than might be thought. Between the two wars the LNER had a number of installations in the North Eastern Area which used a 'transient' track circuit, and before a train was allowed to proceed on to a single line the section was swept by a track circuit current to prove that it was clear. Examples of such installations were: Castleford Old-Ledston 1926, Consett North-Blackhill 1930 and Northallerton-Ainderby 1939.

It is not often that bad weather turns out to have been a blessing in disguise. North of Inverness a single line snakes its way through the remote fastnesses of Northern Scotland over a length of 161 miles, before it finally reaches Wick and Thurso. It is a line which is no stranger to extremes of weather, and in January 1978 a severe blizzard brought down over 40 miles of telegraph wires. It is a line which was on Dr Beeching's list of closures as far back as 1963, and it has hung on since then by the skin of its teeth, thanks to the importance of and the increase in tourism in that part of Scotland. Nonetheless, the cost of replacing 40 miles of telegraph wires would have been a burden that the line could not have sustained and it seemed that its death-knell might have rung at last.

Operators, engineers and boffins from Glasgow and London met to look for a solution. Fortuitously the boffins had been carrying out research into the use of radio as a

Left:
Radio-equipped locomotive No 37261 skirts Loch Carron with the 10.55 Inverness-Kyle of Lochalsh on 19 July 1985. This was the first line in the world to be equipped with Radio Electronic Token Block. W. A. Sharman

communications medium in the regulation of train movements and it was put to them that if they could find a way to convey signalling messages from one signalbox to another by radio instead of by telegraph wire the day might yet be saved. The line, which was single throughout, with loops at stations so that one train could pass another, was signalled by the Electric Token Block system and that would be retained. So far as drivers and signalmen were concerned nothing would change; they would operate the signals and tokens exactly as before. What was needed was a means of conveying the signalling messages as safely and reliably as a telegraph wire. Radio alone could not do this — the transmitter would send out its messages to all and sundry, and the receiver would receive messages from all and sundry on its wavelength. Some form of code was needed, so that the receiver could instantly recognise and act upon messages which were intended for it, and reject all others.

The boffins set to work and quickly produced the solution — a small black box containing a micro-processor for encoding and decoding messages, which was attached to the Electric Token Block instruments. The system was brought into use in August 1980 and has worked effectively. As a spin-off, because an entire radio transmitting system had to be set up to deal with the signalling messages, it became possible to provide a radio link between signalmen and trains on the line. This is particularly useful in view of the long distances between some of the stations, the remote territory through which the line passes, and the effects of severe winter weather which sometimes cause trains to be marooned and lost. Thus at one stroke the line ceased to be a museum piece and leapt to the very forefront of technological progress.

West of Inverness there is another long straggling single line, hanging on to its life even more tenuously than the line to Wick. It leaves the Wick line at Dingwall then threads its way by mountain and loch 63 miles to Kyle of Lochalsh. Both lines were vital links and heavily used in the two World Wars and are evocatively described by Canon Roger Lloyd in his delightful book *Railwaymen's Gallery*. It is also one of the lines so charmingly brought to life in Alexander Frater's Odyssey *Stopping-Train Britain*. But sentiment alone is not enough to keep the line open; if it were the line would be extremely prosperous.

BR, with the Treasury breathing down its neck as usual, were faced with a stark choice: reduce the cost of working the line, or close it. At the same time, by happy coincidence, BR were considering how radio could be used to reduce the cost of working another line, which too was struggling to survive — the 48 miles long double track East Suffolk line between Ipswich and Lowestoft. If that line remained double, would a simple Train Despatching system, with commands transmitted by radio, be safe enough? The idea being developed was known as the 'basic railway'. All train movements on the line would be authorised by a central Controller using radio to give instructions directly to drivers. There would be no signalboxes or signals.

When ready to leave a station, a driver would radio to the Controller, giving his train identity number and the name of the station at which he was standing. He would then request permission to travel to the next station. If the previous train was at least *two* stations ahead permission would be given. All trains would stop at all stations and if the timetable was adhered to, trains would in any case be many miles apart. If for any reason a train lost time or broke down the Controller could be told by radio straight away.

Although this simple system might be acceptably safe on a double line it was not considered good enough for single lines. Train Despatching systems, although widely used

overseas, were outlawed in this country for very good reasons by the 1889 Regulation of Railways Act because they had caused too many head-on collisions. Overseas railways, as we noted at the beginning of this chapter, still have their collisions. At Flaujac in France, 32 passengers were killed in a head-on crash in August 1985 when two passenger trains collided on a single line worked under a Train Despatching system. However, even though a simple Train Despatching system by radio may not be thought safe enough on its own for a single line in Britain, could it form the basis of such a system if some means were found of retaining the concept of the token without requiring intermediate signalboxes for its operation?

Operators, engineers and boffins put their heads together again and pooled their views. The initial idea in the development process was for the token machines to be located on the platforms at stations, and linked together by radio. Drivers would operate the token machines themselves by radio-operated release from the signalman, and take out or replace a token. The Controller would tell the driver whether it was in order for him to take out a token and the equipment itself would ensure, as in normal practice, that only one token for a section could be out at any one time. The disadvantage of this idea was that it would require drivers to leave their locomotives in all weathers to operate the token machines and they might have to cross to the other platform to do it. Technical staff would have to travel to the stations to maintain the equipment.

The next idea was based on the use of a coded card rather like a bank card. The driver would stop his train alongside a card-machine and insert his card to book his train into the single line section. If the section was clear his card would be returned. If the section was not clear his card would be retained until it was, and an indicator would show 'Section occupied'. When the driver passed through the section and

reached the next station he would book himself out of the section. Tokens would not be used, except that the card could be regarded as a token, and the driver would not enter a section if his card were locked in the machine. The card-machines would be connected by radio and a micro-processor would ensure that no card could be returned from the machine to a driver unless the section was clear. The card would be a sort of electronic token. But somehow it did not feel like the ideal solution.

One day an operator and a boffin were having lunch together and musing over the various possibilities. Boffins by their very nature are full of ideas, and bang-up-to-date with the latest wizardry, varying from the highly impractical to the downright ingenious. Unfortunately their lack of down-to-earth practical experience sometimes makes it difficult for them to distinguish between the two. On the other hand operators, beset with practical difficulties, may be having to struggle to cope with them because they just do not know what whizz-bang solutions are being made available by technology and research; or do not recognise their potential because they do not properly understand them. But back to the lunch. 'What we need', said the operator, 'is a means of giving a token to the driver without the signalman actually having to hand it to him. We need a means of doing it remotely. Instructions given by voice alone are not sufficiently safe; there is too much possibility of misunderstanding. We must have something like a token to ensure safety.' 'Would you accept', replied the boffin, 'a radio system in which a centrally-located signalman could send a message to the driver which would then appear on a miniature screen in the driving cab?'

The conversation then went on as follows:

Operator: 'Could it print out the name of the section, say, Dingwall-Garve?'
Boffin: 'Yes.'

Operator: 'And could it be a unique message, so that once it had been given to one driver the same message could not be given to another?'
Boffin: 'Yes.'
Operator: 'And could it ensure that the message went to the intended driver, and not to any other?'
Boffin: 'Yes.'
Operator: 'And could it ensure, as with an electric token, that the signalman could not take back the message from the driver, without the driver's consent?'
Boffin: 'Yes.'
Operator: 'And could the system ensure that the driver couldn't accidentally "give up" the message while still in mid-section, by requiring co-operative action between both the driver and the signalman?'
Boffin: 'Yes.'
Operator: 'So the system could follow the Electric Token principles which we operators know and trust, with the sole difference that there wouldn't be a physical token?'
Boffin: 'Yes.'
Operator: 'Just a sort of electronic one?'
Boffin: 'Yes.'

And so the Electronic Token system was born. The lunch was worth it. The Kyle of Lochalsh line was an obvious one on which to try out the system. It was self-contained, operated by a captive fleet of locomotives and a limited number of drivers who knew that their jobs were at stake; had a sparse train service which could easily be controlled by just one signalman, and speeds were not high. A few moments' delay in carrying out radio procedures at stations would be of no importance. But two vital consequences would flow from the introduction of the system — (1) it would considerably reduce the cost of operating the line and so help its survival, and (2) the act of investment in ultra-modern equipment would be seen by the staff, by

103

local people and by politicians, as an expression of BR's faith in the future of the line. It would be a great morale booster.

The system is based on the well-tried and very safe principles of the Electric Token system. The signalman 'hands' the electronic token to the driver, and for the transfer to be completed both signalman and driver must press a button on their equipment simultaneously. The token will then appear on the driver's console display and he will confirm to the signalman that he has correctly received it.

Instead of a Starting signal then giving the driver permission to enter the section, the signalman will give permission by radio. On entering the single-line section the driver will tell the signalman by radio as soon as the train is clear of the loop of double line at the station. This is important for two reasons — (1) as soon as the line at the loop is clear another train can be allowed to leave the loop in rear, and (2) if for any reason a driver had left a loop and entered the single-line section *without* the signalman's permission the signalman would realise this at once and tell the driver by radio to stop, also the driver of any other train heading towards him, thus ensuring safety.

In order to keep costs down, the points at loops are not worked by the signalman (who is likely to be many miles away) but are spring-loaded so that they always lie towards the same line. They can safely be trailed through by a train leaving the other line of the loop and proceeding in the opposite direction. It is necessary for them to be passed through in the facing direction at low speed as they are not locked, but it is in any case necessary for trains to enter the loops slowly because there are no safety overlaps; a train might be just running into the opposite loop from the other direction. When a train has entered a loop and has cleared the single line and the points, the driver will inform the signalman accordingly by radio. He will also confirm that his train is complete, ie none of it has been inadvertently left on the single line. Signalman and driver will press their buttons simultaneously and the electronic token will be returned to the signalman. The driver's console display will be cleared and the token will appear on the signalman's console display. If the section ahead is clear the procedure for token issue may then be repeated to allow the driver to proceed into the next single-line section. The signalbox computer ensures that tokens are issued in the correct sequence, keeps a record of all trains on the line and prevents the signalman from authorising conflicting train movements.

The Radio Electronic Token Block system, as it is called, is now in operation on the Kyle of Lochalsh line, the Highland line from Dingwall to Wick and Thurso, and the East Suffolk line. Plans are being developed for its installation on the West Highland line to Fort William and Mallaig, also on the line from Aberdeen to Inverness, and on the Cambrian line from Shrewsbury to Aberystwyth and Pwllheli. It is particularly useful for long single lines where the cost of installing the radio system can rapidly be recovered by savings in signalmen and the maintenance costs of lineside signals and signalboxes. There are, however, not really all that many lines of such a nature in Britain — probably not more than a dozen — but the system has enormous export potential, particularly for Third World railway systems. It can also form the basis of more advanced systems which can be applied to either double or single lines, by providing for tokens to be transferred without the train having to be stopped in a loop to do so. The points at the entrance to a loop can be operated, detected and locked by radio command, to avoid the train having to pass through them at low speed. Transponders located in the track can detect the position of the train and announce it by radio to the signalman. Magnetically-coded tail lamps can provide detection that the train is complete. Who knows, it might one day become the standard system on those lines with moderate speeds and a limited train service which do not qualify for full modern signalling with colour-light signals and continuous track-circuiting. The operator and the boffin might yet regret not having patented it!

Right:
On 1 August 1986 No 37415 approaches Fearn with a Wick/Thurso-Inverness service passing a 'Stop' board installed for the recently-introduced radio signalling system. David Brown

Trains without Guards

In 1985 the newspapers were full of reports about BR's proposals to withdraw guards from trains. Readers' letters bemoaned the imminent demise of the passenger guard, women feared for their safety from the attentions of less-reputable fellow passengers, and the leader writers thundered against what they saw as BR's lack of sensitivity and commercial wisdom. Had the newspapers got it wrong? Perhaps they had. It was never BR's intention to withdraw guards from *all* passenger trains but only from selected suburban services. Certainly not from InterCity services. But was the furore partly BR's own fault? Had it presented the proposals as clearly and thoroughly as possible? Had it made clear the limited effect of these proposals? Had it properly explained how safety would be provided for in the absence of a guard? Had it under-estimated the travelling public's desire for a 'railway presence' on passenger trains, even humble suburban ones, in order to reassure passengers in these increasingly violent times; and had it failed to realise how valuable such a 'presence' could be in reducing the loss of revenue from fare-dodging passengers?

BR's presentation of its proposals to its own staff may also have lacked sensitivity and imagination, and may have caused unnecessary unrest and opposition. Guards could be forgiven for gaining the impression that their jobs were to disappear in thousands overnight, rather than in stages over several years. Furthermore, BR may not have appreciated sufficiently the hidden commercial benefit of a railway presence on suburban trains; indeed its provision came about more as a result of trade union pressure for job protection than anything else. The National Union of Railwaymen was anxious to save as many jobs as possible

and persuaded BR to regard as a trial the first scheme for working trains without guards, on the newly-electrified St Pancras-Bedford suburban service. It was agreed that the displaced guards would in the meantime act as Ticket Inspectors on those trains, and they have proved so successful at this that there is a case for such a practice being made permanent. The presence of a railway official on a train is also reassuring to the ordinary passenger. The trend towards the unstaffing of suburban stations and now the unstaffing of suburban trains is at variance with the need to maintain order in an environment that can at times be hostile, and some railway administrations have found it prudent to restore staff to previously unstaffed stations. Whilst this might be regarded as a semi-police function, it is more expedient in a variety of ways to use railway staff, who can carry out other duties as well. There is a strong marketing factor here — railways need to attract passengers, and that requires an attractive travelling environment.

BR had been attempting to introduce guardless trains since technology made it practicable to do so safely and economically by the early 1970s. However, the NUR was implacably opposed to any such moves, reinforced by resolutions at their Annual Conference. Quite naturally the guards were reluctant to see their jobs disappear, but a more astute union leadership might have accepted the inevitable and concentrated its efforts on obtaining the best rewards for all those who would be involved in the operation of guardless trains, whilst at the same time making the best possible provision for those guards displaced. As it turned out, the rank and file of the NUR

Left:
Guardless trains on the Midland: a Class 317 EMU heads through Hendon on the Up Fast line. Top centre is the tv screen angled towards the Down Slow line to enable the driver to check that all is in order to close the doors and depart, whilst just to its right is the tv camera pointing along the platform. Author

finally refused to be led into confrontation, and the operation of guardless trains began, albeit on a fairly limited scale.

So far as BR was concerned, there were those who looked upon the concept of guardless trains as the answer to the railways' economic problems. There were also those, somewhat shrewder, who recognised that a price would have to paid for union agreement to driver-only operation. Extra payments would be demanded by, and conceded to, those who might have to take on extra responsibilities. Costly equipment would have to be provided on safety grounds. The ultimate economy might be considerably less than had been hoped for. But BR had to achieve its ambitions for three reasons: one economic, one operational and one political. The need to make economies in the operation of trains speaks for itself. The operational case is simply that the ability to run trains without guards avoids being forced to cancel trains when no guard is available, a running sore, particularly in the London suburban area, caused by the inability to recruit sufficient guards and the economic necessity of keeping the establishment of spare guards to a minimum. The political case is the most interesting one. BR had to achieve success in its struggle with the NUR over the operation of guardless trains in order to prove to the government that the railway management meant business and that they were determined to comply as far as possible with the government's demand that the railway's dependence on public funds be reduced. It was hoped that the government would then be so delighted with BR's victory that it would release massive amounts of capital to be invested in electrification, resignalling, and the renewal of rolling stock, which is exactly what happened. Sir Robert Reid, chairman of BR, succeeded where Sir Peter Parker, the previous chairman, had failed. He provided a Conservative government with a number of resounding political victories, for which railways (and the railwaymen themselves) were duly rewarded. To be fair to Sir Peter, it has to be admitted that the industrial relations climate favoured Sir Robert, but it was a notable achievement nevertheless. The political acumen of the present chairman is one of his strongest suits. It is fascinating to consider whether the nationalised railways have not fared better under ideologically-opposed Conservative governments than under supposedly sympathetic Labour ones. It is also an interesting thought that if the NUR had not opposed driver-only operation there would have been no political victory and hence no reward. Perhaps after all the NUR leadership were more politically aware than they have been given credit for!

However, turning from the political and economic aspects of driver-only operation to the operational and safety implications, we might start by considering how the use of guards on trains came about in the first place, and why the practice has continued for so long. To find the answer to that question we have to go back to the very beginnings of railways, when they had just started to take over from the stage-coach. The first railway carriages were just like stage-coaches on a railway chassis. Stage-coaches carried guards to help passengers and to look after their luggage, and to assist with braking. It was a natural development therefore that railway carriages, modelled on stage-coaches, should have guards to do those things. One of the most important of the guard's duties in the days before continuous automatic brakes was to assist the driver to brake the train. This often required a number of guards and brakesmen, but when trains became fully braked they were no longer needed for that purpose. However, by then, guards had become an integral part of the working of trains and were retained. There was never much justification for having a guard on fully-fitted freight trains (ie trains which

are fully-braked throughout with the brakes on the whole train being operated by the driver) in steam locomotive days when there were always two men on the footplate.

The guard traditionally sat at the back of a freight train in his brakevan ('sat' is a euphemism — the guard braced himself in his seat and wedged himself as best he could as protection against the shocks, bumps and lurches of a normal journey). On a loose-coupled freight train, in which the wagons were coupled together by a simple three-link coupling which allowed a gap of a foot or so between the buffers of adjacent wagons, and which had no power brakes other than those on the locomotive, the guard had a number of important duties:

1 He used the handbrake in his van (called appropriately a brakevan, not a guard's van) to assist the driver to keep the train under control on falling gradients.
2 He used his handbrake to keep the couplings taut when travelling over undulating gradients, thus avoiding snatches which could lead to the breakage of a coupling. This was quite a skilful job on a 100 wagon freight train, which might be on two or three different gradients at the same time.
3 If the train accidentally broke into two portions when running, the driver would often be unaware immediately that anything untoward had occurred, but the guard would be there to bring the rear portion safely to a stand if he could. If the rear portion became derailed, the guard was in a position to protect the opposite line if it was obstructed by derailed wagons (and to protect his own train).

A guard on a loose-coupled train was a vital member of the train crew and absolutely essential. An experienced and capable guard could be of great assistance to the driver, although inexperienced and clumsy ones could be a nuisance to the driver, who might then say to the guard 'Leave the braking to me'. However, on fully-fitted freight trains there was no need for the guard to carry out any of these duties — the wagons were screw-coupled together so that the buffers were touching and the driver controlled the power brake on every wagon. In the case of a coupling breaking or an accidental uncoupling (rare events on such a train) the automatic brake would bring both portions to a stop without any action on the driver's part. Hence the name automatic brake. If for any reason the rear portion had become derailed the fireman could have looked after it in the absence of a guard. However, fully-fitted freight trains always carried a guard, who sat at the back ready to rush off with his flag and detonators in the event of an accident. The LNER actually went so far as to move the brakevan inside the train to ease the operation of dropping off or attaching a few wagons at stations en route, but with the stipulation that there must not be more than 20 wagons behind the brakevan.

With the advent of diesel haulage, needing only one man on the locomotive, the position is somewhat different, but before we go on to examine the effect of that on proposals to withdraw guards, let us see how the use of guards on passenger trains developed. The continuous automatic brake had become standard on all passenger trains before the turn of the century and it was rare for the guard to have anything to do with the brake during a journey. His duties developed in three main spheres, which are largely unchanged today — the safe and expeditious working of the train, commercial duties in relation to his passengers (called 'customer care' nowadays), and responsibilities for the safe carriage of mails and parcels.

The passenger guard's operating duties are mainly:

1 To see that his train is in good order before departure.
2 To satisfy himself, in co-operation with the driver, that the brake is working satisfactorily.
3 To see that all doors are closed before departure.
4 To 'protect' the train in case of accident, and look after the passengers.

The first three items arise before departure. The train should be in proper order before it leaves its depot, and station or depot staff are capable of carrying out all 'station' duties. It is when the train is out on the line that situations may arise to cause problems on guardless pasenger trains. If the train were to break down the driver would have to leave it unattended whilst he went for assistance. If it became derailed, and obstructed other lines, the driver could only protect one direction at once. If it caught fire the driver alone could not protect the train, go for assistance and look after the passengers. Whilst these might be thought to be remote dangers there would certainly be a lessening of safety standards if guards were to be removed without any additional compensating safeguards being applied, and this would be unacceptable in the launching of a new method of operation that would demand acceptance by the travelling public, the staff, the trade unions and of course the Railway Inspectorate of the Department of Transport. BR therefore drew up the following conditions to be applied in the operation of guardless suburban passenger trains:

1 Doors are to be power-operated by the driver.
2 Automatic Warning System (AWS) equipment must be provided.
3 If a platform is not manned, drivers must be able to obtain a clear view of the platform along the full length of the train.
4 Radio communication between driver and signalman must be provided.
5 The line must be track-circuited throughout its length.

These five conditions form the main requirements. Taken together they may provide an even higher standard of safety than applies with conventional train working. The driving of the train is unchanged, but the driver has the benefit of AWS and continuous track circuiting. So far as accidents are concerned, he is in constant radio touch with the signalman and he could, at least in theory, alert the signalman and so secure the safety of the line even *before* an accident, in the following manner. Normal radio calls from the driver to the signalman are dealt with in rotation but the driver has an emergency button and if he were to press it the signalman would be alerted at once. Details of the train would appear on the signalman's radio console and the signalman could ascertain from his diagram panel just where the train was. He could then put out a general radio call to all drivers in the area to tell them to stop (or proceed cautiously) and he could put the protecting signals to Danger. Thus, before the train concerned in the emergency could come to a stand, and long before the driver could telephone for assistance or use his track-circuit operating clip, as he would have to do on a conventional train, all trains in the area would have been warned and would themselves be coming to a stand. Safety would then be achieved much more quickly than under present conditions.

The question of the operation of doors on trains was dealt with at length in Chapter 5. On a guardless train, as there is no guard to see that all doors are closed before departure, nor to take action if anyone should attempt to join or alight just as the train is setting off, power-operated doors under the control of the driver are necessary. It is also necessary that the driver should be able to see along the full length of the train so that he can tell when it is reasonable to close the doors (for example he would not want to do it just as an infirm passenger was being helped in or out, nor when someone was just lifting a pram in or out), and so that he can be sure that no one is trapped in the doors. There is a general safeguard that, unless the doors are properly closed, an interlock will prevent traction power being applied to the train and it will be unable to move, but a scarf or strap may not be detected by the interlock and anyone so trapped could be dragged along the platform when the train started. Unless the driver can see clearly along the platform, means must be provided to enable him to do so. These take the form either of television cameras sighted along the train, with a TV screen on the platform opposite the driver's cab or, in suitable cases, a large mirror on the platform to enable him to see round the outside of a slight curve, or to see along a platform on the right-hand side of the train. If the circumstances are such that the driver cannot look back in safety as the train leaves a station, because of the presence of an overbridge or tunnel for instance, emergency stop plungers must be provided on the platform, for use by station staff or passengers if there are any present. This may be thought to be over-doing things a little, because the driver will have checked before he sets off that everything is in order and it assumes that someone is going to place himself in an irretrievable position of danger in the next two or three seconds. However, for a new venture such as guardless trains it is better, for purposes of public and staff acceptance, to be too safe rather than not safe enough. The requirements can always be relaxed in subsequent schemes if experience shows that they are unnecessary.

One of the more intriguing requirements stipulates that the driver's safety device (DSD), more popularly known as the 'deadman's handle', must not be capable of being neutralised whilst the train is in motion. On some stock the DSD can be rendered inoperative by the driver putting his 'forward/reverse' power controller into the 'engine-only' position, allowing him to coast along without having to depress the DSD pedal. It is strictly forbidden whilst the train is on the move but it is known to be done occasionally for various reasons. If it were to be done on a guardless train and the driver were to become insensible, a dangerous situation would arise. This requirement prevents it from being done; if the 'forward/reverse' controller is put into the 'engine-only' position at any speed above walking pace, the brake is automatically applied.

A public-address system is provided on guardless suburban passenger trains so that the driver can give any necessary instructions to passengers in an emergency, as well as making routine announcements. Consideration is also being given to a means of allowing passengers to speak to the driver. Whilst this could be misused by irresponsible passengers it would help to reassure law-abiding travellers, who could draw the driver's attention to unruly or intimidating passengers, enabling the driver to radio for police attendance at the next station. This would be far more effective than the passenger having to pull the communication cord, resulting in the train being brought to a stand away from a station and away from assistance.

The thought of a fire on a passenger train is always frightening, and although no passenger has been killed in a fire on a suburban passenger train for very many years, and although there is often little a guard could do in such a situation, it is necessary on guardless trains to provide an escape-route for passengers. Through access must there-fore be provided between all coaches forming a multiple-unit, and passengers must be able to open emergency exit doors (whether end or side doors) from within the train. But with radio on the train, and public address, the situation

can be dealt with much more effectively than on a conventionally-manned train. The driver can radio for fire brigade assistance and stop his train at the most suitable point. In the meantime he can give the passengers whatever directions are most appropriate. The signalman will have stopped all trains, so that passengers jumping out of the affected train will not be in danger of being run down by other passing trains.

The question is often asked as to what would happen if the driver were to become insensible whilst driving, or be put out of action in a crash. In the first case the operation of the DSD would bring the train to a stand, and in addition the AWS at any Caution signal or severe speed restriction would automatically cause the train to be stopped. So far as the effects of a crash are concerned, the driver would almost certainly have time to press his radio 'emergency' button so that the signalman could take immediate protective measures. Furthermore the radio system is so designed that the signalman can speak to the passengers over the train's public address system. On a conventional train there is no guarantee that the guard will survive a crash and even if he is not killed he may be injured to such an extent that he cannot carry out his protective duties, a possibility that has always been accepted because it is unavoidable. On fully track-circuited lines, if debris from the crash obstructs another line it is likely to short-circuit the track-circuit on that line, which will automatically put the last approaching signal to Danger, and alert the signalman if he is not already aware of the emergency.

As a result of all these special arrangements, the operation of guardless passenger trains is very safe indeed; safer than many conventionally-manned trains. However, it is a costly venture and the pay-back is not as brilliant as might be thought. The balance sheet of costs and benefits is as follows:

Capital costs:
Provision of radio system and equipment.
Provision of CCTV or other equipment on station platforms.

Additional running costs:
Maintenance of additional equipment.
Extra payments to drivers and signalmen for extra responsibilities.

Savings:
A proportion of the guards' costs. (Some will still be required for ticket inspection and customer-care duties.)

Benefits:
Overall reduction in running costs.
A safer, more efficient service.
A more reliable service.
More productive use of manpower.

As guardless suburban passenger trains have not been operated for long, it is too early to assess the economic results of the arrangement, but it is to be hoped that BR will publish them in due course so that an informed judgement can be made. There are of course a number of imponderables. How much extra revenue will on-train ticket inspection produce? How many extra passengers will be attracted by a 'railway presence' in the passenger accommodation of the train? How much extra business will be generated by the increase in the efficiency of the service by the provision of radio, and the avoidance of the need to cancel trains when there is no guard available? The eventual verdict is likely to be a resounding vote of confidence in favour of the operation of guardless suburban passenger trains, but BR must take care to present the full facts so that the public can be reassured.

The position of ASLEF (the Associated Society of Locomotive Engineers and Firemen — the drivers' trade union) in this matter is interesting. During the long negotiations (10 years or more) they have kept a very low profile. They have not suggested that the proposals were in any way unsafe (as NUR did) nor that the drivers would be unable to carry out the extra duties. They made a number of sensible detailed suggestions about the equipment to be provided. What they were chiefly interested in was the pay-off — how much extra money could they obtain for the extra work and responsibility; a very proper consideration for a trade union. But a cynic might remark that ASLEF was not losing any members, whereas the NUR was, and trade unionism is partly about the number of members. Falling numbers make it more difficult for a trade union to maintain an efficient administration, with good research facilities. The world of industrial relations becomes increasingly complex day by day, both in the technical and legal senses, and a trade union needs an expensive organisation to deal with it efficiently. ASLEF, being a small union, is particularly vulnerable in this respect.

The strict requirements for the operation of guardless suburban passenger trains, especially those concerning power-operated doors, radio and continuous track-circuiting, will have the effect of extending the period of the introduction of such workings over several years whilst the existing slam-door stock is replaced by power-operated door stock and sufficient funds are made available for resignalling and the installation of radio. So far, guardless suburban passenger trains only operate on the lines from King's Cross and St Pancras, and from Glasgow to the Ayrshire coast.

The safety requirements for the operation of freight trains without guards are naturally rather different in concept from those of passenger trains. Many of the problems associated with passenger train working do not arise, but there are other factors to be considered which are confined solely to freight train operations. Whilst the term 'freight train' will be used throughout, the arrangements also apply to parcels, mail and newspaper trains, empty coach trains and light locomotives. All trains must be fully-fitted, with the automatic brake operative throughout the train. Trains which have Post Office staff or newspaper sorting staff on board are regarded as passenger trains and are excluded from these arrangements.

The operation of freight trains has always been carried out at a safety level which, whilst not so high as that for passenger trains, was considered to be adequate but which did not, indeed could not, provide for every eventuality. In theory the guard observed the running of the train and took action to have it stopped if he observed anything untoward. In practice both his view, and his opportunities for observation, were very limited. He could not see much in the dark, his view along the train from the lookout windows of his brakevan was very restricted, and at speed the guard was often preoccupied with wedging himself in his seat to avoid being thrown around the van by its poor riding qualities. The number of occasions in actual practice when guards have initiated action to have their trains stopped, and have thus prevented a possible derailment, have been few. In the mid-1960s BR decided to abolish the use of brakevans on most fully-fitted freight trains, and place the guard in the rear cab of the locomotive where he could still observe the train. It caused a lot of industrial relations problems. The NUR felt that it reduced the status of the guard and suspected that it was the first step towards doing away with guards altogether. ASLEF felt that the sanctity of their domain, which they jealously guarded, was being infringed. However, the arrangement was finally adopted, but guards can often be seen travelling with the driver in the *front* cab. In freight train collisions in which the driver is killed or injured it is noticeable that the guard often suffers the same fate alongside him.

The other reason for having a guard on a freight train has traditionally been to protect his train and secure the safety of the line in case of accident or breakdown. The protection of his own train is much less vital nowadays with modern signalling and improvements in signalling controls, and the driver is responsible for protecting the line used by trains running in the opposite direction. On four-track sections the guard may have to protect the other line running in the same direction as his own train if it has become obstructed by wreckage, but most four-track sections nowadays are track-circuited and can be protected just as effectively by the driver using his track circuit operating clip. In any case, experience has shown that the guard's actions have rarely had any practical effect in avoiding a subsequent collision or reducing its effects.

In drawing up the safety requirements for the operation of freight trains without guards BR were particularly concerned about two factors — the propensity to derailment of short-wheelbase four-wheeled wagons, and the carriage of dangerous goods. During the 1960s and early 1970s the problem of derailments of what were at that time the standard wagons and vans became very serious. The vehicles concerned had a wheelbase of about 10ft and formed the great bulk of BR's wagon fleet, and many of them had been built since nationalisation. For reasons never really satisfactorily explained, derailments started to occur in freight trains travelling at about 50-55mph, a situation which had never previously been experienced. The number of such derailments increased year by year, each one ending in a pile of wreckage, and there was the ever-present fear that one day a passenger train would run at full speed into the heap of tangled metal and shattered wood. Fortunately there were very few really serious accidents involving passenger trains[1], but occasionally a second freight train ran into the wreckage, and once or twice a third freight train added itself to the heap. On one memorable occasion on the Erewash Valley main line of the former Midland Railway north of Toton, a coal train on the Up Fast line became derailed and the wreckage was run into by a train of iron ore on the Down Fast line. A third train on the Slow lines joined in. Fortunately there were no serious injuries but there was a heap of coal, wood, iron ore and scrap metal big enough to start up an ironworks. Both Derby and Toton breakdown cranes were engaged for 24 hours. The explanation of the cause of such derailments was often the same — a combination of minor faults in the wagon suspension (usually within agreed engineering tolerances), minor faults in the track (again usually within tolerances), and the speed of the train at or slightly above the maximum allowed. It was an unsatisfactory conclusion because there seemed to be no remedy, except the drastic one of reducing the speed at which the wagons were allowed to travel. This came down in stages from 60mph to 55mph, to 50, then to 45mph. Even this did not fully solve the problem and 16-ton coal wagons had finally to be restricted to 35mph. The effect on transit times was disastrous and a great deal of traffic was diverted to road by dissatisfied customers, especially after National Carriers Ltd was formed following the 1968 Transport Act. The solution to the derailments was never really found and it will always be a mystery as to why wooden-framed wagons could run happily at 60mph and above when hauled by steam engines on jointed track composed of 60ft rails laid on wooden sleepers, whilst the same wagons with steel frames could not be trusted to stay on the rails at much above 35mph when hauled by diesel locomotives, especially on long-welded rail laid on concrete sleepers, but it has

something to do with the greater flexibility and 'give' of wooden-framed wagons on jointed track on wooden sleepers, compared with the stiffness of steel frames on concrete sleepers. The problem was finally solved (or solved itself) with the replacement of the wagons by longer-wheelbase, higher capacity vehicles with improved springs and suspension, and with the reduction in freight traffic which allowed many wagons to be scrapped without replacement.

When the requirements for the operation of guardless freight trains were being drawn up, the derailment problem was still very much a live issue and it was decided that short-wheelbase wagons (defined as having a wheelbase of less than 15ft) should not be allowed to run in guardless trains except on continuously track-circuited lines with multiple-aspect signalling, so that if a derailment occurred it could be protected by the driver using his track-circuit operating clip, and there would be a signal-post telephone nearby from which he could report the derailment to the signalman. Longer wheelbase wagons, which are much less prone to derail, are allowed to run in guardless trains on non-continuously track-circuited lines as well as on those which are continuously track-circuited, but only where there is not a frequent passenger train service (not more than two per hour in each direction). There is no special precision or particular logic in this; safety is an art as well as a science and the running of guardless trains is a new art form. It is felt better to be more restrictive to start with, until some experience has been gained. The full requirements are listed in the appendix, and include details of those dangerous goods for which a guard must be provided. Once again it was felt prudent to be cautious in entering the untried area of the operation of freight trains without guards, when such trains are conveying goods of a dangerous nature. There are some types of dangerous goods which are hazardous in an unusual way, such as nuclear flasks containing irradiated fuel rods, or particularly toxic chemicals conveyed in tank wagons. On trains conveying such dangerous traffics a brakevan will continue to be provided at the rear of the train and a guard must travel in it, so that if the train has an accident the traincrew need not, indeed must not, walk alongside it in case of possible health risks from any leakage of the contents.

Radio communication between driver and signalman could be a useful aid in certain circumstances on guardless freight trains, but that applies also to trains with guards. It is not specially a matter of safety but rather one of expediency. A case for additional safety equipment can always be made out from a purely safety point of view, but the expenditure has to be justified in terms of the balance of probability. It is right and proper to spend money to guard against a hazard which can reasonably be foreseen, but it would be an extravagance to use limited funds to guard against an unknown or indefinable hazard, or one which may never happen.

Finally we should consider the economics of the operation of freight trains without guards. Apart from minor modifications to locomotives, the balance sheet shows a pure gain for freight trains running between yards, sidings and depots where there are BR or other suitable staff to carry out all the necessary terminal duties such as:

1 Placing the wagons on arrival.
2 Informing the computerised freight traffic control system, known as TOPS (Total Operations Processing System).
3 Uncoupling the locomotive.
4 Coupling the outgoing train, checking that it is fit and safe to travel, and noting any restrictions.
5 Informing TOPS.

6 Placing a tail lamp on the rear wagon.
7 Coupling the locomotive.
8 Carrying out the brake test.

The driver could certainly carry out some of these duties at unstaffed sidings, for which he would probably want extra pay, but there are technical problems in carrying out a brake test single-handed. More importantly, is it sensible to have a million pounds' worth of locomotive and wagons, to say nothing of their load, standing idle whilst the driver performs such duties? A judgement has therefore to be made as to whether it is more advantageous to carry a guard in certain cases, or even to employ terminal staff at previously unstaffed sidings. Each case has to be judged on its own merits.

Appendix 1

Conditions for One-Man Operation of Suburban Passenger Trains on British Railways

Rolling stock

Doors
Side doors to be power-operated and controlled by the driver. Interlock to be provided with the traction controller so that the train cannot be moved unless all passenger doors are closed.

Traction and braking control equipment
A form of driver's safety device, which the driver cannot neutralise whilst the train is in motion, must be provided.

Application of the brake must automatically cut off the traction power.

Automatic Warning System equipment must be provided, unless train stops are provided.

Through access between coaches, and emergency exit doors
Stock is to be fitted with end doors giving access between coaches within a unit, and between units where practicable.

Passengers must be able to open emergency exit doors from within the coaches. These may be either end doors or a proportion of the side doors on each side of the train, or both. Opening of the doors is to be effected by conspicuously-marked, sealed-release handles or buttons. If only end doors are available as emergency doors, passengers must be able to get to either end of the train.

Train equipment
Track circuit operating clips shall be provided in each driving compartment.

Stations

Platform lighting
Platforms must be adequately and uniformly illuminated.

Manning of platforms and use of CCTV (closed circuit television)
If a platform is not manned, drivers must be able to obtain a clear view of the platform along the full length of the train. If necessary CCTV or other means may be provided to achieve this.

Emergency stop plungers
Where circumstances are such that the driver cannot look back in safety as the train leaves the station, emergency stop plungers are required on the platforms for use by station staff and passengers. Operation of an emergency stop plunger shall illuminate emergency Stop signals ahead of the platform and beyond any Starting signal.

Communications

Driver to signalbox or control
A system of continuous direct speech communication shall be provided between the driver and the signalbox, or a control centre in direct communication with the controlling signalbox, for the section of line in which the train is located.

Public address
A system of driver-to-passenger speech communication must be provided.

Signalling

All lines over which one-man operated suburban trains run in passenger service must be continuously track-circuited. This includes any adjacent running line that could be fouled by a derailed one-man operated train.

AWS must be provided.

Appendix 2

Conditions for One-Man Operation of Fully Fitted Non-Passenger Carrying Trains on British Railways

Rolling stock

Automatic brake
The automatic brake, either air or vacuum, must be operative throughout the train in conformity with the appropriate regulations.

Traction and braking control equipment
A form of driver's safety device which the driver cannot neutralise whilst the train is in motion must be provided.

Application of the brake must automatically cut off the traction power.

Train equipment
Track circuit operating clips shall be provided in each cab or driving compartment.

Signalling

Trains that include vehicles with a wheelbase of less than 4.5m
May run over passenger lines that are continuously track-circuited and equipped with three- or four-aspect colour-light signals, and over goods lines or loops adjacent thereto. May also run over non-continuously track-circuited passenger lines for short distances (up to 10 miles depending on circumstances) at the beginning or end of a journey, or intermediately, and also without restriction on single lines and on goods lines where these are not adjacent to passenger lines.

Trains composed of bogie stock or vehicles with a wheelbase of 4.5m or over
May run over the lines described above and in addition may also run over non-continuously track-circuited lines where passenger traffic is light (not more than two booked passenger trains per hour in each direction).

Light locomotives (single or in multiple)
May run over any line.

Traffic restrictions

The following dangerous goods must not be conveyed on one-man operated trains:

    Flammable gases in tank wagons, Class 2a.
    Toxic gases in tank wagons, Class 2c.
    Hydrocyanic acid.
    Explosives, Class 1.

[1] At Ashchurch on 8 March 1969 a 16-ton mineral wagon in a 57-wagon freight train from Birmingham, Washwood Heath, to Bristol, Stoke Gifford, became derailed only seconds before an express passenger train (the 10.40 Bristol-Newcastle) passed in the opposite direction. The coaches of the express were severely damaged by derailed wagons and two passengers lost their lives.

Obstructions on the Line

One of the perennial concerns of drivers is that of running into unprotected obstructions on the line. The driver cannot swerve and he will probably be too near to stop, especially if the obstruction is round a curve. In the darkness he will have no chance at all. There are many types of obstruction, but the ones we shall be concerned with in this chapter are:

Animals on the line.
Goods fallen from passing trains.
The effects of bad weather, eg fallen trees, snowdrifts, rock-falls, mud-slides.
Lorries and other vehicles running off the road.
Vandals.

Animals on the Line

It can be said that the railways have always had a duty to fence the line, going back to the 1842 Railway Regulation Act and beyond. This duty was to prevent cattle from straying on to the railway from adjoining land, and to prevent trespass *from* the railway. It was not originally intended to safeguard children from straying on to the railway and unwittingly putting themselves in danger, although it has come to be interpreted as such. There are about 20,000 miles of fencing alongside the railways of Britain, costing about £6 million a year to maintain. Some of the expenditure arises from damage caused by children, or by adults seeking a short cut.

The Rule Book tells drivers that if they see animals on or near the line, which they consider may endanger trains, they must tell the signalman as quickly as possible, and take other safety precautions. Since June 1986 the Rule Book has specifically said that a cow or bull or other large animal must be considered a danger to trains. The signalman, in turn, must stop trains and tell the drivers what has happened, and instruct them to take their trains forward cautiously. In this way subsequent trains are safeguarded.

Top:
The scene after the crash at Watford Junction on 23 January 1975. The driver of No 86209 survived his terrifying plunge down the embankment. British Rail

Above:
No 86209, the locomotive of the 22.15 Euston-Glasgow sleeper, seen where it came to rest at the foot of the embankment. The locomotive was to remain there for nearly three months, whilst the difficult operation to retrieve it was organised. British Rail

Each year there are thousands of instances of animals, mainly sheep, straying on to the line or on to the grassy area at the lineside, and many of these instances go unreported. However, about a hundred times a year trains run into animals on the line, and occasionally, once or twice a year, there is a derailment. Serious derailments are rare. Human fatalities are almost unknown. That was the case until Monday 30 July 1984.

The 17.30 express from Edinburgh to Glasgow that evening consisted of a Class 47/7 diesel-electric locomotive pushing six coaches. The leading vehicle had a driving compartment from which the locomotive and train were remotely controlled. Shortly after passing through Polmont, and whilst travelling at about 85mph, the train hit a cow and became completely derailed. The first coach turned right round and finished up on its side, and several other coaches were badly damaged. The behaviour of the coaches after the impact has interesting parallels with that of the coaches involved in the Lockington accident described in Chapter 12, as has the way in which fatalities occurred when passengers were thrown through the windows. Altogether 13 of them were killed and 17 passengers and railwaymen were seriously injured. In terms of fatalities it was BR's worst accident since the Hither Green derailment in 1967, when 49 passengers were killed.

Human trespass in the area was common and the fencing had to be repaired frequently. It is thought that the cow had gained access through a fence damaged by trespassers, and this problem of fence damage and trespass is very difficult to control, not only at Polmont but almost anywhere on BR. It is certainly not within the realms of practicality to prevent animals from getting on to the line, therefore BR took action in a number of directions after the accident, such as improvements to the Rules, the fitting of deflectors (cow-catchers) to Scottish Region push-pull trains and the equipping of driving cabs with radio to enable drivers to give early warning of animals on the line, or to be warned accordingly by the signalman.

Goods Fallen from Passing Trains

Once again the West Coast main line, and a sleeping car express, figure in these pages, in an accident that happened on 23 January 1975. The 22.15 sleeping car express from Euston to Glasgow was settling down to a steady speed of about 85mph on the approach to Watford Junction when the signals suddenly went to Red in front of it. The driver made an emergency brake application and had managed to reduce speed to 65mph when he suddenly saw looming up in front of him the bulk of another electric locomotive which had obviously been derailed and was leaning over towards him. He had hardly time to hang on tightly and pray that he would miss it, when the two locomotives struck each other a glancing blow, corner to corner, and his

Left:
The recovery of No 86209 involved the use of two 125-ton capacity cranes on 16 April 1975, with spreader beams to protect the locomotive's bodyside panels. A full account of the recovery of No 86209 appeared in the June 1975 issue of *Modern Railways*. Sparrows Crane Hire

Above:
The severely damaged remains of the leading locomotive of the Manchester-Euston train, Class 83 No 83003, being jacked up before removal. British Rail

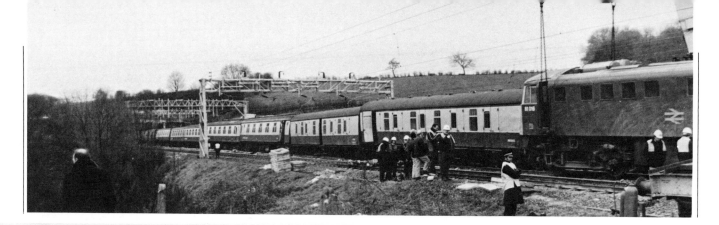

Top:
Class 81 electric No 81016 being rerailed after the accident near Leighton Buzzard on 9 December 1982. David K. Smith

Above:
A view of the derailed coaches in the Leighton Buzzard accident. David K. Smith

locomotive cannoned off and shot down the embankment to the left. He was very lucky to survive his appalling ordeal, but the driver of the other locomotive was killed. Fortunately the sleeping cars became detached from the locomotive and did not follow it down the embankment but came to rest more or less in line along the track.

The cause of the derailment of the other train, the 19.10 express from Manchester to Euston, was clear. Some steel stillages had fallen from a passing freight train and had lain foul of the Up Fast line, on which the express from Manchester was just accelerating from its booked Watford Junction stop. It ran into the obstruction and was derailed towards the Down Fast line, but in doing so it cut the signal cables of the track circuits in that line, causing the signals to go to Danger in the face of the fast approaching sleeping car express. Had both trains met at full speed, ie at a combined speed of almost 200mph, the result would have been catastrophe on a grand scale. But accidents are always full of 'ifs'.

The train from which the steel stillages had fallen was company train No 6M50, the 20.12 from Fords of Dagenham to their Halewood plant. All the van doors had been secured and sealed before the train left Dagenham, but when it made a routine stop at Rugby for a crew change several van doors were found to be open. How could this have happened? They could not have worked open on their own during the journey because they were too well fastened. It was then found that the train had stopped twice for signals

in the north London area, at Gospel Oak and Finchley Road, and police investigations led to the conclusion that the train had been attacked there by thieves, who had left the doors open. Vibration of the train during its journey then caused two stillages to fall out of the van just south of Watford Junction, to be run into by the express from Manchester. The cause of the accident was really a form of vandalism, although the robbers probably never thought of the possible consequences of their actions. Whether they would have been deterred had they done so is another matter.

Sleeping car expresses, and the West Coast main line, seem to occupy more than their share of the limelight in these pages (do they really suffer from a disproportionate number of accidents?) and by coincidence the same train was involved in another accident in the small hours of Thursday 9 December 1982. The express, now timed to leave Euston at 22.25, had left two hours late because there had been a defect in the electric train heating system. The train had just passed through Leighton Buzzard, travelling at about 75mph on the Down Slow line, when the electric locomotive, No 81016, ran into a steel rail which was thought to have fallen from an earlier engineering train. The derailed locomotive hit a bridge parapet, killing the driver and injuring the secondman. Twelve of the 14 coaches were derailed but stayed upright and in line. Only one passenger was injured.

The Effects of Bad Weather

The night of 9 December 1982 was extremely stormy in the south of England, with fierce winds and lashing rain. As the 21.46 electric multiple-unit train from Waterloo to Bournemouth was travelling at 90mph near Fleet (Hants) it ploughed headlong into a pine tree which had been blown over on to the line. It was BR's second train crash within 24 hours (the other one was near Leighton Buzzard, just described).

The train careered along for half a mile with the leading

vehicles derailed but fortune favoured the hundred passengers, none of them being hurt, although they had a very frightening experience. The driver was slightly injured but not detained in hospital. He said, 'We had a very lucky escape. It was pitch black, when suddenly there was a tremendous bang and the train started to bump all over the place. It seemed ages before we stopped.'

Lorries Running off the Road

The driver never knows where or when he will encounter an obstruction, and one of the hazards he has to contend with is that of cars and lorries running off the road on to the railway. Such an event, which cost the engine-driver and his mate their lives, happened in the small hours of 15 March 1976 near Annan, between Carlisle and Dumfries, when the driver of an articulated lorry attempted to negotiate a bridge carrying the A75 road over the railway. The lorry collided with the parapet and fell on to the railway line. At this stage the nearest approaching train was still 10 miles away, but by the time the alarm had been raised the train, the 20.55 express from Euston to Stranraer, had passed the last signal at which it could be stopped and its diesel-electric locomotive No 47274 crashed into the lorry at almost 80mph. None of the passengers was hurt but the lorry driver, who was later found to have three times the permissible amount of alcohol in his blood, was killed.

The Department of Transport have now recognised this particular hazard, and crash barriers have been erected at the sides of roads in locations where the railway could be imperilled.

Vandals

This cause of accidents stands out from all others in a number of ways. In the first place it is a misnomer to call the results of vandalism an accident; vandalism is a deliberate act where the perpetrator is either ignorant of the possible consequences of his actions, perhaps doesn't

Above:
The two locomen and the lorry driver all died in this accident near Annan on 15 March 1976 when the lorry ran off the road at an overbridge. K. S. McQuade

care, or in extreme cases really intends that those consequences should happen. In the second place it is so difficult to guard against.

Astonishingly, many of those carrying out acts of vandalism are too young to be prosecuted, or not much older. A few, thankfully only a tiny minority, are so wildly reckless in their actions that their soundness of mind must be questioned.

On 16 February 1979 a crowded HST from Paddington was travelling at about 65mph just beyond Reading when it ran into two lengths of rail which had been placed across the Down Main line in such a manner that one of them was angled upwards towards the approaching train. The vandals must still have been nearby when the HST hit the rail because it was the evening peak and the intervals between trains were short. We shall never know what the vandals hoped would be the outcome of their actions, nor whether they deliberately set out to derail the train with reckless unconcern for the deaths and injuries which might result, but even they must have been unprepared for the spectacular consequences of their actions. The upturned rail split the fuel tank of the leading power car, and immediately fire broke out, enveloping the first three coaches in flames before the train could be stopped. However, the fire did not penetrate the coaches and rapidly died out and the train was not derailed. Those who committed the outrage were never caught. It is thought that they must have had some railway knowledge because they managed to place the pieces of rail across the line without short-circuiting the track circuit, and they may have been people with a grudge against BR; perhaps former employees who had been dismissed.

A piece of rail was also used in another vandal attack

115

upon the railways on 22 May 1980. An Up sleeping car express on the East Coast main line had just left Edinburgh and had reached almost 70mph nearing Prestonpans, when it struck a piece of rail nearly 6ft long and weighing about 2cwt. The rail bounced along beneath the train with an enormous clatter, nearly frightening the sleeping car passengers out of their wits, until eventually it distorted the track and derailed all the coaches after the third one. They remained fairly upright and in line and there were no serious injuries. On this occasion the culprit was found — a 17-year old youth, who was committed to Borstal. History does not reveal whether this reformed him, but it certainly did not deter others — in 1985 six trains were derailed by vandals and there were 179 cases of trains running into obstructions, almost half of which were of railway material, mainly left behind after renewal or repair. So, at least part of the solution is in BR's own hands.

Below & bottom:
Derailed sleeping cars after the train had run into a piece of rail placed on the track by a vandal at Prestonpans on 22 May 1980. Iain M. Flynn

But lest it be thought that vandalism against railways is a recent social disease, it is apparent that our forefathers were also troubled by it. The Midland Railway Rule Book of 1883 even went so far as to quote part of the 1861 Offences Against the Person Act:

'Whosoever shall unlawfully and maliciously put or throw upon or across any Railway, any Wood, Stone or other Matter or Thing. . . with Intent to endanger the safety of any Person travelling upon such Railway, shall be guilty of Felony, and being convicted thereof shall be liable to be kept in Penal Servitude for Life, or for any Term not less than Three Years, or to be imprisoned for any term not exceeding Two Years, with or without Hard Labour, and if a Male under the age of sixteen years, with or without Whipping.'

The law is still in force today, although the penal servitude, hard labour and whipping have been replaced by simple imprisonment. It is often difficult to prove 'intent to endanger', especially in the case of younger people, but even without such intent the Act provides for two years' imprisonment. So the law is strict enough; catching the vandals in the first place is the difficulty.

Automatic Open Crossings

Not all the hazards that drivers have to face arise in the day-to-day signalling and operation of the railway. There is another category of hazard which may arise wherever railway and road cross each other on the level, and it introduces to our story another type of driver — the driver of a road vehicle.

1986 will not be remembered as a good summer, but the East Coast had the best of the weather and Saturday 26 July was fine and sunny there. In Bridlington station, the 09.33 stopping train to Hull, formed of a pair of two-car diesel multiple-units, was loading up with holiday-makers on their way home to Hull, some looking back on the enjoyment they had received, others looking forward to the familiar surroundings of home. None had any apprehension of possible danger in the relatively short journey ahead; after all, this was a quiet line with no high speeds so why should there be any cause for concern?

The train left Bridlington on time and set off on its 31-mile, 49min journey. At 09.55 it stopped at Hutton Cranswick station and after a few moments went on its way again. Everything was as normal as could be.

Three miles further down the line, at the closed station of Lockington, everything was normal too. One of the occupants of the railway cottages there saw her next-door neighbour climb into his blue Ford Escort van, as he did every Saturday morning, and set off towards the lane at the bottom of the station approach road. His route then took him over the level crossing at the old station.

The 09.33 train from Bridlington, now with about 120 passengers on board, approached the level crossing at almost full speed — between 60 and 70mph. At the controls its driver had no inkling of imminent disaster. Why should he? The line from Hull to Bridlington and Scarborough was peppered with level crossings and he had driven over it for

years. But that morning the malign hand of fate was working. It was not going to be another routine journey after all, neither for train driver nor for van driver, whose paths were destined to meet on the level crossing.

The train, weighing well over 100 tons, struck the van squarely in the middle and smashed it to pieces, scattering them far and wide, then careered on for 150yd before leaving the rails. The first coach reared up and turned completely round on itself, hurling passengers to their deaths through its broken windows, whilst the remainder of the train jack-knifed itself across the tracks. It was no longer a routine journey. Altogether eight passengers died, and 37 were seriously injured. A little boy of 11, a passenger in the Ford Escort van, also lost his life. It was one of Britain's worst-ever accidents at level crossings, equalled only by the one at Hixon, between Stoke-on-Trent and Colwich, on 6 January 1968, when an express from Manchester to Euston crashed into a heavy transporter lorry carrying an electrical transformer. Hixon level crossing had been modernised the previous year and automatic half-barriers with flashing red road traffic signals had been installed.

There were no automatic half-barriers at Lockington level crossing; only flashing red lights. This type of crossing at Lockington, known as an automatic open crossing (AOC)*, was devised by a working party of British Rail and Department of Transport experts in 1978 and the first one was installed in 1983 (at Naas, between Newport and Gloucester). Automatic open crossings were seen as a cheaper alternative to the automatic half-barrier crossing (AHB), the first one of which had been installed at Spath, on the now-closed line from Uttoxeter to Leek and Ashbourne, in 1961. By the end of 1985 there were 291 AHB level crossings, and 39 AOCs on BR.

Left:
The scene at Lockington after the train from Bridlington to Hull ran into a motor van on the automatic open level crossing. The van was almost totally destroyed by the force of the impact, whilst the two diesel multiple-units forming the train were completely derailed, with the leading vehicle turning through 180° before coming to rest.
The Press Agency (Yorkshire) Ltd

*Technically known as an AOCR — automatic open crossing remotely monitored. There is another type of crossing known as an AOCL — automatic open crossing locally monitored.

The text on signs in the image:

Drivers of LARGE or SLOW VEHICLES must phone and get permission to cross

LARGE means over 55' long or 9·6" wide or 32·5 tons total weight SLOW means 5mph or less

PARK HERE AND USE PHONE AT CROSSING

ANOTHER TRAIN COMING if lights continue to show

KEEP CROSSING CLEAR

KEEP CROSSING CLEAR

It might be appropriate at this stage to describe briefly the equipment and method of working of these two types of level crossings, which apart from the half-barriers are very similar. They are illustrated on pages 118-121 and consist of warning lights (amber and flashing red), and various traffic signs. There are no gates but AHB crossings have a lifting barrier which, when lowered, closes off half the road on the left-hand side. The warning sequence is initiated automatically by an approaching train when it occupies a track circuit designed to be long enough to give the necessary warning time of 27sec for trains travelling at the maximum speed allowed for that particular section of track. The amber light glows steadily for 3sec, followed by a minimum of 24sec of flashing red. At an AHB crossing the barriers descend after the lights have been flashing for 8sec.

Such times, measured in seconds, might be thought to reduce safety margins to an unacceptable level, but in fact there is no point in providing longer margins, which would merely encourage impatient car-drivers to 'jump' the lights. In theory there is no reason on safety grounds why the train should not go over the crossing as soon as the rear of any vehicle which is too near the crossing to stop when the amber light shows has passed clear of it. For this purpose 27sec is generally ample time, but the arrangement does mean that it is quite possible for people in a car to look down the line when going over a crossing and see a train approaching, even though the warning lights were not operating when the car passed them. This can give rise to incorrect allegations that the lights have failed.

The working of the crossing equipment is continuously monitored by a nearby signalbox, where there is an indicator to show that the main electric power supply is available at the crossing. So far as AHBs are concerned there is another indicator in the signalbox to show when the barriers are raised. AOCs have an in-built warning system that gives an audible alarm in the signalbox if all the red lights facing in one direction fail. At both types of crossing there is a telephone to the signalbox. An audible warning sounds at the crossing as soon as the amber light shows, but this is for the guidance of pedestrians, not vehicle drivers.

Above:
Britain's first automatic open crossing at Naas, between Newport and Gloucester, commissioned in 1983. At each side of the crossing there is a telephone connected to a signalbox. The cross and chevron above the flashing lights tell the road user that there are two railway tracks, although it is highly questionable whether many road users understand the meaning of this sign. British Rail (WR)

Right:
A typical automatic half barrier installation. British Railways

AHBs and AOCs may be provided on any railway line with not more than two running lines (a term which denotes lines other than sidings), but the maximum speed of trains over the crossing must not exceed 100mph for AHBs and 75mph for AOCs. The speed and volume of road traffic is of no consequence at an AHB but at an AOC it must not exceed 2,000 vehicles per day. Furthermore, the total number of road vehicles per day at an AOC multiplied by the total number of trains per day must not exceed 40,000, nor more than 600 in the peak hour. There is nothing magic or scientific about these figures — they are purely arbitrary and designed to reduce the chances of a train and a road vehicle being on the crossing at the same precise moment if something has gone wrong or someone has made a mistake. The limitation to 75mph is designed to reduce the effects of a collision if the one-in-a-thousand chances turns up. At Lockington it did turn up and even at 60-70mph caused devastation.

Automatic level crossings are not interlocked with railway signals and such signals may show Clear whether or not the lights are flashing, and irrespective of the presence of a road vehicle on the crossing, but there must be a signal capable of being placed at Danger not further away than 10min running time for the fastest train. This is not only to allow trains to be stopped in case of emergency but also to allow abnormally heavy or slow lorries, or herds of animals, to cross the lines safely by telephone arrangement with the signalman.

Automatic crossings are capable of being switched to non-automatic operation when necessary, for example when one of the tracks is being repaired, or when nearby road works may cause vehicles to tail back on to the crossing. In such cases a railwayman will be stationed at the crossing, and he will operate the barriers and lights manually. Trains approaching the crossing will be stopped by the signalman and the drivers will be warned to approach the crossing cautiously and not to proceed over it until they have received permission from the man at the crossing that they may do so. Operations of this nature, the details of which are not known to road users, may sometimes give rise to stories and rumours that the lights were seen not to be working properly, or that they had failed.

The advantages of automatic level crossings may be summarised thus:

1 They avoid failures of the human element on the part of railway staff employed to operate crossings with gates. Fatal accidents occasionally occur at such crossings.
2 Gated crossings often have railway signals protecting them. Trains sometimes crash through the gates when the driver inadvertently slides past the signal, and if there happens to be a road vehicle in the way the results can be disastrous for its occupants.
3 Automatic crossings avoid the heavy manning costs associated with gated crossings.
4 The flow of road traffic is speeded up. Automatic crossings are closed for less than a minute when a train passes; gated crossings for three or four minutes because it is necessary to swing the gates across the road and clear the railway signals in time to give a clear indication at the Distant signal to an approaching train which may be up to 2 miles from the crossing. If the signal is not at Clear when it comes into the driver's view he will slow down ready to stop at the signal at the crossing, which may cause it to be closed to road traffic for longer than normal.
5 When trains pass over a level crossing at short intervals, either from opposite directions or where one closely follows another, the interval between the trains may be too short to allow the gates to be swung open (or manned barriers to be raised), thus the gates or barriers may have to remain closed across the road whilst two or even three trains pass. The delay to road traffic can be considerable, especially if a long queue builds up, as it does in the rush hour at busy crossings. Automatic crossings go a long way towards solving this problem — they will open between trains even if only 10sec is available before the next train 'strikes in' and triggers off the warning lights.

There are, of course, disadvantages. Automatic crossings are safer than *some* gated crossings, but they are not

necessarily safer than manned level crossings provided with full-length lifting barriers and flashing road traffic signals, nor with such crossings unmanned but monitored remotely by closed-circuit television. One of the less desirable effects of automatic crossings is that they may be said to transfer the responsibility for safety at the crossing from trained and reliable railway staff to road users who may occasionally act recklessly, irresponsibly or carelessly. It could be argued that if the road user wants to kill himself by his own stupidity, so be it, but that philosophy is only tenable so long as those actions do not endanger the lives of railway passengers. And of course it is not always a question of stupidity; it may be a simple failure of the human element.

In this connection we must make a distinction between AHBs and AOCs. It is hardly possible for a road user to cause a collision at an AHB crossing through carelessness or lack of attention — the half-barrier sees to that. It can only be caused by stupid recklessness. Not so at an AOC, however. There is no half-barrier to wake up the day-dreaming car-driver, and the stupid driver can 'jump' the lights without the tell-tale zig-zag round the barriers. But all this was foreseen when AOCs were devised, hence the limitations which were imposed.

But let us now return to Lockington. Was there a system failure at the crossing? It seems very unlikely indeed. Two witnesses saw the red lights flashing normally as the train approached the crossing, although they were on the opposite side of the crossing to the Ford Escort van driver. Nevertheless, it is technically inconceivable that the lights should flash normally in one direction and fail completely in the other, and yet be found to be in proper working order when tested afterwards. Furthermore such a failure would have sounded an alarm in the monitoring signalbox. No such alarm was received; and it must be said that wrong-side failures of level crossing automatic equipment are very rare indeed.

Perhaps we shall never know exactly what happened at

Below:
A poster issued in 1962 in connection with the installation of an automatic half barrier level crossing at Stallingborough on the line between Barnetby and Grimsby. Note that early crossings of this type had only the two flashing red lights.
British Railways

Below right:
A modified version of the automatic half barrier crossing, installed at Ripe, Sussex, in 1970. New features included an amber light giving advance warning before the flashing red lights. The illuminated message 'Another Train Coming' denotes the passage of another train before the barriers rise.
British Rail

Lockington. The van driver, the one man with the key to the explanation, was badly injured in the crash and it often happens in such circumstances that the memory of those moments preceding the accident is blurred or completely erased. However, there are a number of important factors peculiar to this case, which go far to render it untypical.

In the first place the van driver lived in the railway cottages almost next to Lockington level crossing. Although the crossing had only recently been modernised he can hardly have been unaware of it. It cannot have been the case that he suddenly came upon it and was confused by its method of operation. Secondly the van driver did not approach the level crossing by driving straight along the road towards it; had he done so he would have had the benefit of all the warning traffic signs, plus the full 24sec of flashing-red road traffic signals. The two witnesses previously mentioned gave evidence of how visually-arresting the lights were. But the van driver did not have the benefit of the warning traffic signs, nor a good long view of the flashing lights; on the contrary he turned on to the lane leading over the level crossing only a few yards from it. In such circumstances, especially if pre-occupied at the start of a journey, might it not be possible to overlook the lights, especially if they were in view for only a few seconds against a bright sky background?

There is another consideration too. Experienced car drivers do not concentrate consciously on every aspect of their driving. On the contrary, much of it is done as an automatic reaction. We do not consciously say to ourselves 'I am approaching a left-hand bend, therefore I must turn the steering wheel in an anti-clockwise direction'. We do not say to ourselves 'I have now accelerated to 30mph on the level so it would be appropriate for me to change from third gear to fourth'. No, for much of the time car driving is done on 'automatic pilot', because the procedures have been so completely absorbed. Consider therefore someone who has regularly driven over a gated crossing. His mind is then programmed: 'Gates across the road. I must stop, as there is a train coming'. If the gates are not across the road his mind is equally programmed 'No train coming, it is safe to cross'.

Let us then apply this philosophy to the events of the morning of the accident and let us surmise as follows: The van driver set off on his journey, turned on to the lane and approached the crossing. His driving was on 'automatic pilot'; perhaps his mind was pre-occupied. His 'automatic pilot' was programmed to look for gates across the road. There were no gates across the road so the reaction of the automatic pilot was to drive over the crossing. The warning lights, visible only for a few seconds, did not penetrate the consciousness. It must be stressed that this is only a surmise, but it is a possible explanation of events.

But if we accept the surmise for the sake of argument, what does it prove, and what considerations flow from it?

In the first place we have already concluded that the circumstances of the accident were untypical and we ought not to condemn automatic open crossings on the basis of this one accident alone. On the other hand, though, if the 'automatic pilot' theory is accepted it would surely have detected the presence of a lowered barrier at an AHB crossing and the driver would have stopped clear, so we might therefore conclude that AOCs are unsuitable but AHBs are acceptable, *but only in the special circumstances of the Lockington accident*. That consideration would not apply to the normal user of an automatic open crossing because the visual impact of red flashing lights for up to 24sec would surely penetrate the consciousness and overcome the automatic pilot, even without the presence of a lowered barrier. It must be accepted, however, that AOCs are marginally less safe than AHBs; that has always been the accepted view, hence the restrictions on their use.

There are a number of other advantages that AHBs possess over AOCs. There is always a temptation to a reckless or impetuous road user to jump the lights, and it is easier to achieve at an AOC, where a driver may sneak across hoping he will not be noticed, whereas at an AHB it is necessary to do a very obvious zig-zag round the lowered barriers, which also entails going over the double white line and possibly reducing speed, an undertaking likely therefore to deter all but the most foolhardy.

Another advantage of AHBs concerns the situation which arises when a second train approaches the crossing just as the first train has cleared it. A day-dreaming car driver switched on to automatic pilot might well set off over the crossing as soon as the first train has passed, even though the lights are still flashing, but would hardly drive through a lowered barrier. It has to be admitted therefore, that it would be easier to set off unwittingly over the crossing at an AOC than at an AHB, even though a flashing sign is provided at AOCs which reads 'Another Train Coming'. This possibility too was recognised when AOCs were devised, hence the restriction on the combined volume of trains and road vehicles, which helps to reduce the number of occasions when two trains pass over a crossing in quick succession. It should be noted that the lights will cease to flash (and the barrier will rise at an AHB) if the road can be opened for at least 10sec before the approach of the second train triggers off the warning lights.

It might be argued that AOCs are as safe as AHBs when properly used, but this ignores the day-to-day realities of the situation and in practice AHBs are safer than AOCs. The retort might then be 'So what? Are we to have the same standard of safety equipment at *every* level crossing regardless of the degree of peril and regardless of cost?' If the answer to that question is 'yes', then we should have full-length manned barriers at every level crossing because that is what such an answer would entail. But where is the logic in such a demand? And apart from that, why should we demand a much higher standard of safety at a place where rail crosses road than we do at a place where road crosses road? There are many busy, dangerous crossroads which do not even have traffic lights, and even the busiest, most dangerous crossroads do not have barriers with a man to operate them, nor even half-barriers, nor have local

residents ever demanded that they should be so equipped. So we ought not to apply double standards. The type of equipment to be provided at a railway level crossing should be appropriate to the degree of peril, and it would be illogical to act otherwise. But consequent upon that decision is the need to accept an occasional accident without causing an uproar and setting up special government reviews, which happened after the Hixon accident and has happened again after the Lockington crash.[1] It is understandable that the government may wish to calm people's fears about safety at level crossings but it might also be thought of as an insult to the integrity and professional competence of railway managers and a reflection on the standing and independence of the Railway Inspectorate of the Department of Transport.

Finally, the question arises as to the future of automatic level crossings. AHBs have been in use since 1961 and they have been widely installed. There is sufficient experience to indicate that they are acceptably safe in most situations and the site conditions for suitability are strict and clearly defined. Their acceptability was confirmed both by the Inquiry held by Mr E. B. Gibbens QC into the Hixon accident in 1968 and by the joint BR/Railway Inspectorate team which re-examined the question in 1978, and studied continental practice, where the automation of level crossings, both with and without barriers, has proceeded much further than in Britain. However, even continental practice is not perfect. The French Railways had their own 'Hixon' in July 1985 when a push-pull express from Le Havre to Paris, being propelled at nearly 100mph, ran into a lorry on an automatic level crossing at Saint-Pierre-du-Vauvray. Seven passengers were killed and 55 injured. The crossing was equipped with four half-barriers, which British practice has always considered undesirable and potentially dangerous.

Wrong-side failures of equipment at AHBs in Britain are very rare and most accidents are caused by motorists zig-zagging round the lowered barriers. This is a deliberate act and whilst the motorist is at liberty to risk his own life he should be deterred with all the force the law can command from hazarding the lives of innocent railway passengers. Perhaps he should be charged under Section 34 of the Offences Against the Person Act 1861, which provides that any unlawful act, 'which endangers the safety of persons conveyed on the railway shall be a misdemeanour, punishable by imprisonment for two years', rather than be charged under the Road Traffic Acts with a traffic offence and receiving a small fine.

So far as automatic open crossings are concerned, it is too early yet to judge whether they are acceptably safe because they have only recently started to be installed, and there were only 47 of them in use at the time of the Lockington accident. The events at Lockington were not wholly typical but inevitably the accident, being so serious, has brought the question into prominence. BR might have been able to take a relaxed attitude in the days when a heavy steam locomotive at the head of a train could be expected to toss aside any car that got in its way but it is not a valid attitude today, as was so tragically demonstrated at Lockington when a small van succeeded in completely wrecking a

Top & above:
Lockington level crossing looking east, the scene of one of Britain's worst-ever level crossing accidents on 26 July 1986.

100 ton train. And it is not just DMUs and push-pull trains which are at risk. On 4 May 1982, the 13.35 express from Glasgow to Aberdeen, hauled by a heavy main-line diesel-electric locomotive, collided with a farm trailer on a field-to-field farm crossing of private occupation status at Nairn's Crossing near Forteviot, just south of Perth. The whole train, except the last coach, was derailed, and most of it plunged down an embankment into a field, but no one was killed and only four passengers were seriously injured.

The crux of the argument between AHBs and AOCs really boils down to a question of cost. AHBs are acceptably safe. AOCs are less safe than AHBs, but they may still be acceptably safe in certain circumstances. They are somewhat cheaper, but does the saving justify the reduction in safety? Or to put it another way, is the increase in safety of an AHB worth the extra cost? There is no definitive answer.

There are just two other matters to be dealt with. After an accident such as this, the question is always raised as to whether some form of guard or cow-catcher at the front of the train would have avoided the derailment. It is a question that has been raised many times but has rarely been seriously considered. However, after the Polmont accident on 30 July 1984, when an Edinburgh-Glasgow push-pull express being propelled was derailed after running into a cow, resulting in 13 passengers being killed, a form of deflector was designed and fitted to such trains in Scotland. The front-end design of locomotives and multiple-units, and of the first vehicle of push-pull trains, needs to be re-examined to see whether they can be made more resistant to derailment after colliding with road vehicles at level crossings or with heavy animals or objects on the line.

The second matter is really one of clarification. There is another type of automatic open crossing, known as an

Within the image, the following labels appear:

LOCOMOTIVE

TRANSFORMER FROM LORRY

REAR OF TRANSPORTER

WRECKED SIGNAL BOX

CAR

TRACTOR

TRANSPORTER

LEVEL CROSSING

AOCL (automatic open crossing locally monitored) where safety is monitored by the driver of an approaching train. There is no difference in equipment or operation so far as the road user is concerned, but the train driver is required to approach the crossing at such a speed as will enable him to stop safely short of the crossing if it is obstructed when it first comes into his view. There is no telephone from the crossing to a signalbox and the train driver himself checks that the flashing red warning lights are working by observing a duplicate flashing light (white) at the side of the line. The speed of trains must not exceed 55mph but in practice speeds are usually lower. The experience of Lockington brings into question whether the speed limit of 55mph is too high, bearing in mind that the train involved at Lockington was only travelling about 10mph faster than that and if Lockington had been an AOCL the collision would still probably have happened. The speed of 55mph, selected by the 1978 Review team, is purely arbitrary, based partly on continental experience and partly on the excellent safety record at AOCLs before 1978 when the limit was 35mph. Perhaps 45mph would be a suitable compromise — it would have little practical effect on day-to-day operations and would improve safety margins.

As a postscript to this question of safety at automatic open crossings, it is interesting to reflect upon another accident at a level crossing just a mile north of Lockington, almost exactly 10 years earlier. This accident happened on 20 June 1976 at Kilnwick level crossing, when the 09.30 passenger train from Hull to Scarborough, consisting of seven diesel multiple-unit coaches, ran into a saloon car. The car driver was killed but it is notable that although the train was travelling at its maximum speed of 70mph, only its front bogie was derailed and no one on the train was hurt, yet in almost identical circumstances at Lockington 10 years later nine people died and many were injured. It would therefore be unreasonable to attribute the death-roll to the automation of Lockington level crossing, and thereby to condemn the whole principle of the automation of level crossings. There could just as easily have been a similar death-roll at Kilnwick, which at that time was not automated but was equipped with gates, worked by a crossing keeper (at the subsequent Public Inquiry he was

Above:
Hixon Crossing 1968: the scene of chaos after the 11.30 Manchester-Euston express struck a transporter carrying a 120-ton transformer on 6 January. Keystone Press Agency

found to be not at fault). The number and severity of casualties in a railway accident are purely a matter of luck, and safety measures should always be directed at the causes of accidents and their *potential* consequences, not the actual ones.

One final point — Lockington might well be considered a perfect example of a level crossing eminently suitable for conversion to an automatic open crossing; there are only a handful of road vehicles and two trains per hour, the approach road is straight and level and leads to nowhere in particular, and the traffic is local in character, yet a mile up the road there is a situation of much greater danger where the lane crosses the busy, high-speed main road from Hull to Bridlington, which is full of cars, coaches, and 38-ton six-axle articulated lorries, all travelling (some illegally so) at 50-70mph; and there are not even any traffic lights. Such a dangerous situation would not be tolerated on the railway for an instant.

At the time of writing, neither Major King, the Inspecting Officer who held a Public Inquiry into the cause of the accident, nor Professor Stott has issued his Report. But the fact remains that safety at automatic open crossings is largely dependent on the actions of road users. Railway passengers are entitled to expect safety standards to be applied by trained and reliable railway staff and not to be at the mercy of any Tom, Dick or Harry driving a road vehicle. On those grounds automatic open crossings ought not to be used by trains travelling at high speeds. Above about 45mph half-barriers ought to be provided.

---

[1] A committee has been set up by the Department of Transport under the chairmanship of Professor Stott with the remit 'To review the safety record of automatic open crossings, to consider the lessons gained from the experience so far, and to make recommendations to the Secretary of State for Transport.

Conclusions

Anyone reading the preceding chapters may be forgiven for concluding that rail travel in Great Britain is not as safe as its reputation would suggest and certainly not as safe as it could be. The evidence presented in this book could lead to a conclusion that the railways have often been slow to apply remedial safety measures, that deliberations have lacked a sense of urgency, that design work, testing and implementation have been unduly protracted, and that action when finally taken has been half-hearted and reluctant, giving the impression that BR didn't really believe that it needed to do anything. But would such a judgement be unduly harsh and unfair? It cannot be denied that, on the evidence, it has often in the past been a question of too little and too late. One must hope that this is no longer the case, but there is still much to be done in the interests of greater safety, and there can be no standing still.

However, protracted or not, there is no doubt that the actions which BR have taken over the years have borne fruit — in the late 1970s and early 1980s there were four individual years (1976, 1977, 1980 and 1982) in which no passengers were killed in train accidents. In 1983 only two were killed, whilst 1985 was another clear year. In the 10 years 1976-1985, 45 passengers lost their lives in train accidents on BR, which is about as many as are killed on Britain's roads in two or three *days*, and fewer than died in one single airline disaster at Manchester Airport in 1986. The Transport Act 1962, which sets out BR's duties, merely says that the British Railways Board should have *due regard* to efficiency, economy and *safety of operation*. No doubt the draughtsman of that Act found it as difficult as others have done to lay down precise safety standards. Absolute safety is unattainable in practical terms.

There are, however, other considerations. Apart from any

Below:
The old ... Class 47 No 47712 *Lady Diana Spencer* passes beneath the semaphore gantry on the way out of Stirling, heading the 11.05 Aberdeen-Glasgow service on 25 August 1984. W. A. Sharman

moral duty not to kill passengers there are commercial and business implications. A serious collision these days might not cause any passenger deaths but can cause millions of pounds worth of damage. Those same coaches whose design has contributed so greatly to the saving of lives in an accident are in consequence very expensive. So is the track, the signalling and the overhead electrified line equipment. The interruption to the train service may last for days, which causes not only an immediate loss of revenue but also mars the railway's reputation for reliability. And even though passengers might not be killed many are injured, some very severely; and drivers are often killed. So what more ought to be done?

By comparison with continental railways BR has lagged behind in a number of areas: in the provision of radio communication between drivers and signalmen, in equipping coaches with power-operated doors, but most of all in equipment to help the driver. The reasons are partly financial — continental railways receive far more money from their governments than BR does — but there are others. The splendid safety record during the late 1970s and early 1980s did much to strengthen a feeling within BR that a sufficiently high safety level had been reached and that little of a major nature remained to be done. There was also a certain rigidity of attitude that saw no need to do anything more to help the driver, 'He's paid to obey signals' was an oft-heard saying, but as the use of AWS became more and more widespread, signs began to emerge that the concept of the system, being merely advisory, had an inherent flaw. Nonetheless, flawed though it is, AWS has been, and still is, of enormous value, but in the 30 years that have elapsed since the present system was finally approved, technology has moved on and there are now more effective systems available. There is an amply-demonstrated and over-riding need for BR to do more to help the driver and it should tackle the problem with vigour, with determination and, above all, with urgency. It will take several years for such action to bear fruit and in the meantime there could be more accidents, more deaths and injuries and more destruction. One can only hope that BR will not allow sectional interests and short-term pressures to deflect it from the pursuit of such an objective.

To return to the two questions with which this chapter opened: Is rail travel as safe as its reputation suggests? and is it as safe as it could be? To the first question the answer must be 'yes'. BR's reputation as a safe means of transport is deservedly high (despite occasional lapses). The record speaks for itself. To the second question the answer has to be 'no'. To give any other answer would be to fly in the face of the evidence in this book. But there is a third question — *ought* rail travel to be safer? There is no apparent commercial need; BR's current safety levels attract passengers rather than deter them (although that might be a reflection on the competition rather than a credit to the railway). Would substantial investment in increased safety attract more passengers? It seems unlikely. So where is the pay-off? Why should BR spend some of its precious funds on greater safety, for no competitive gain, rather than on improved stations, faster trains, more luxurious coaches, etc, which would improve its competitive position? I believe that the reasons why it should might be summarised as follows:

1 Another accident of the 'Colwich' type could well result in a long casualty list. BR would then be forced to take action.

2 The public's expectation of safety levels will not remain static. It never has done.

3 The Department of Transport will continue to expect a gradual improvement in safety standards.

4 The Health & Safety at Work Act 1974 requires a high standard of safety. Commercial matters are not a factor in the reckoning.

5 Higher speeds will demand a more effective safety system.

6 A more advanced safety system would avoid the cost of double-manning of trains running at more than 100mph.

7 The cost of junction signalling would be reduced.

8 Millions of pounds would be saved by the reduction in the number of serious accidents.

9 The expenditure on improved safety, though substantial, would be spread over many years.

The long saga of accident prevention on Britain's railways has shown generally continuous, although somewhat uneven, improvement and progress. Throughout this history the Railway Inspectorate of the Department of Transport (and its predecessors) have acted as the guardians of public safety. Their conclusions and recommendations, following inquiries into accidents, have most often been accurate and appropriate, indeed, if any criticism can be levelled at them it is that they have not always in the past pressed their recommendations as strongly as perhaps they ought to have done. Theirs is a hard task, and they have a fine line to follow between on the one hand making over-extravagant demands and on the other having too much regard for the railway's financial difficulties. On balance, though, they have carried out their responsibilities with skill and distinction and their reputation is high. Their published reports on accidents are models of narrative layout, clarity and logic, and my only complaint is that they are absurdly expensive — the Wembley Report, published in February 1986, cost £4.90 for just 12 pages and a couple of diagrams, which goes far towards defeating the whole purpose of issuing public reports, if the public don't buy them because they are too expensive. Few railwaymen will purchase them at that price, yet they are the very people who ought to be buying and studying them.

As our story has unfolded in the preceding pages it is uncanny how often sleeping car expresses have figured therein, sometimes even the same ones, yet they form only a small proportion of the total number of express trains. It can only be coincidence? The West Coast main line south of Crewe has also been frequently mentioned but here there is perhaps a more logical explanation — it does have the reputation of being BR's busiest main line. Yet its rival, the East Coast main line south of Doncaster, has hardly had a mention.

And finally, so far as the individual passenger is concerned, he or she need have no fears about safety, despite all that I have written. Even on the basis of a daily journey to and from work a passenger would have to live for many thousands of years to have an even chance of being killed in a train accident. So take heart, and continue to travel by the most comfortable, most enjoyable and safest means of transport ever devised. Generations of railwaymen have dedicated themselves to seeing that it is so.

Below:
... and the new: a multi-aspect colour-light signal in the Glasgow area. GEC

Index